Built on the Sand

Built on the Sand

Biblical Solutions to the Crash of Church Attendance

BRIAN BLACK

RESOURCE *Publications* • Eugene, Oregon

BUILT ON THE SAND
Biblical Solutions to the Crash of Church Attendance

Copyright © 2021 Brian Black. All rights reserved. Except for brief quotations in critical publications or reviews, no part of this book may be reproduced in any manner without prior written permission from the publisher. Write: Permissions, Wipf and Stock Publishers, 199 W. 8th Ave., Suite 3, Eugene, OR 97401.

Resource Publications
An Imprint of Wipf and Stock Publishers
199 W. 8th Ave., Suite 3
Eugene, OR 97401

www.wipfandstock.com

PAPERBACK ISBN: 978-1-7252-9350-2
HARDCOVER ISBN: 978-1-7252-9351-9
EBOOK ISBN: 978-1-7252-9352-6

03/09/21

Contents

Chapter 1	Crisis in the Church	1
Chapter 2	Denominational Difficulty	10
Chapter 3	Contrasting the Models of Church Growth	18
Chapter 4	Necessity of the Power of God	25
Chapter 5	The Sociological Causes of Church Growth	33
Chapter 6	The Necessity of Evangelistic Theology	43
Chapter 7	Why Strict Groups May Fail	49
Chapter 8	Biblical Foundations for Growth	57
Chapter 9	Identifying the Mission Field	63
Chapter 10	Evangelism in a Postmodern World	70
Chapter 11	The Biblical Method of Growth—Part 1	81
Chapter 12	The Biblical Method of Growth—Part 2	89
Chapter 13	Defining Growth	97
Chapter 14	The Answer for the Church	106
Chapter 15	The Answer for the Holiness Movement	119
Chapter 16	Hope for the Future	132
Bibliography		139

CHAPTER 1

Crisis in the Church

The church in America is headed for collapse because its foundations are being destroyed. Some of the ideas regarding church growth are sucking the very lifeblood out of our movement. For a time some of these ideas seemed to be spectacularly successful, but it came at the expense of the future. These philosophies regarding growth not only have undermined and destroyed key doctrinal beliefs, but are now also causing numerical collapse. Many churches are on life support. Others have died. The reproductive power to plant and establish new churches has disappeared. What has happened? The entire spectrum of the evangelical movement is suddenly struggling. Evangelical Baptists, Pentecostals, and Holiness denominations were exploding with vigor and power in the mid-twentieth century. The movement was like a young athlete running with the sheer joy and excitement of life. With his bursting energy, he believed he could overcome and conquer the world.

One example is the Church of the Nazarene. This church, after its beginning in the 1908 merger at Pilot Point, Texas, averaged more than 100 percent membership growth per decade for three decades.[1] The original membership of 10,414 in 1908 blossomed to 301,675 souls in fifty years.[2] Nazarenes also had a burning drive to start new Holiness churches in every town across America. The original 228 churches in 1908 had grown to 4,587 churches in fifty years.[3] Between 1848 and 1956, Nazarenes added more

---

1. Purkiser, *Called Unto Holiness*, 2:303.
2. Purkiser, *Called Unto Holiness*, 2:303.
3. Purkiser, *Called Unto Holiness*, 2:303.

than 1,000 churches to their number.[4] Something has happened, however; membership growth rates began to slow by mid-century and continued dropping almost every decade, down from 114 percent in the mid-1930s to 12 percent in the 1990s.[5] In the decade from 2005 to 2015, the Church of the Nazarene declined in actual numbers in the United States and Canada.[6] Statistics from the Baptists and other Holiness denominations show similar patterns of growth and then difficulty. The Pentecostals have not begun yet to decline in actual numbers but are following the same pattern. Thankfully, this is not true on the mission field for many denominations, such as the Nazarenes; unfortunately, at home, the youthful energy and power are gone. The decrepit body of what is left of many local churches better fits the nursing home than the athletic field. For many, it is too late for the hospital; the undertaker must be called. America is quickly heading the way of the European church, where Christianity has almost completely died. Those who are taking the vital signs are viewing the emergency situation with alarm. There is a fearful crisis which has brought on a desperation within church leadership circles for growth. Yet, the harder denominations have worked at the job, the more it seems like they are failing.

The example given here is of the Church of the Nazarene, but an equal example could have been used of the Southern Baptist Church. This denomination grew about 40 percent during the 1940s and 1950s, growing from a denomination of 5 million to a denomination of 9 million. Its growth continued, but at an ever-slowing rate until it topped out at more than 16 million members about 2005. Since that time its membership has begun to shrink.[7]

The Assemblies of God would be another example, growing about 60 percent during the forties and fifties, but its growth has declined to less than 10 percent in the last decade. The Church of the Nazarene lies in my heritage, and to me there was no greater group than those men and women who had the glory and fire of God burning in their soul and a fervent passion for the lost to be saved. My heritage in the Holiness movement and back to the Methodist Church is the best for which one could ever ask.

If one has a background in the Baptist church, they should be equally proud of the way the Baptists impacted America and helped take our country for God. They should appreciate the stand for the Bible that the Baptists and those of the Reformed theology took defending the fundamentals of the Christian faith in the battle for the word of God earlier in the twentieth

---

4. Purkiser, *Called Unto Holiness*, 2:225.
5. Purkiser, *Called Unto Holiness*, 2:218.
6. http://nazarene.org/statistics.
7. http://www.thearda.com/Denoms/D_1087.asp.

century. Those who are associated with the Pentecostals should be excited by the impact they have had in America and worldwide throughout the last century. Nevertheless, a person cannot live in the past; this is our day, and the church has lost its power. As David lamented over Jonathan and Saul in 2 Samuel 1, we too could say, "How are the mighty fallen." Our prayer should be that God would restore his people.

NEED FOR AN ANSWER

The question is "Why?" What has happened? If the church of today does not come up with the answers, there is no future. Unfortunately, the current answers given out to the church world are often not producing results, but in some instances are the source of the problem. Evangelism today has moved from intercessory prayer, conviction of sin by God, and a transformational conversion, to a seeker-sensitive model of church growth which focuses on being culturally accommodating. These two models of growth are in conflict in many ways. One teaches a kind, gentle approach, while the other drives to the heart of one's sin and demands change.

These things are not written to condemn, but to bring the church to a stark realization that the church is in serious trouble. "Make no mistake. We as Bible-believing evangelical Christians are locked in a battle. This is not a friendly gentleman's discussion. It is a life and death conflict between the spiritual hosts of wickedness and those who claim the name of Christ."[8] The goal is not condemnation, but action to restore the church to what it was. In many ways the church is doing things right. We are aggressively applying ourselves to evangelism, and the Bible is emphasized and preached. Let us continue to be effective with what we are doing, but build upon a lasting foundation. We must have revival throughout all of Christianity; therefore, I am directing this book to all Bible-believers who are looking for answers. We must call the church to repentance; this is the example of Christ who condemned the sin in the Jewish world of his day in no uncertain terms and preached repentance. This is also true of many of the great revivals of history which first called the church to repentance. The repentance was then followed by a powerful move of God in converting the lost in society.

The church in America can have a new awakening. There are clearly answers found in God's word and backed up by modern scientific studies. The question is whether a person will accept these concepts or stick his head in the sand, as the proverbial ostrich, and keep working at the failed system, wondering why the results are never any different. Accept the challenge;

---

8. Schaeffer, *Great Evangelical Disaster*, 31–32.

study the principles given in this book. Although a person may initially disagree with these concepts, study them for yourself. These principles have been proven; yet much more work needs to be done in expanding and applying these concepts into a working system which will change our world.

Jesus told a story of two houses in Matthew 7. In this story, one man built his house upon the rock, and the other man built his house upon the sand. When the storm came it struck both houses, and the one which was founded upon the sand collapsed, while the one built upon the rock stood firm. The same is the story of church growth today.

Long-term, lasting growth comes when a church builds upon a firm foundation. If a church is built upon personality, programs, entertainment, or any other false foundation, it will eventually collapse. For a church organization to continue to grow, year after year, it must be built on a solid foundation. Building on the sand may bring spectacular short-term success, but it will not last. Furthermore, others, seeing the temporary success of churches built upon the sand, may exchange their solid foundation for that which will collapse as well.

Christianity in America is in serious decline. The number of people who self-identify as Christian is dropping rapidly. In 1980, 89 percent of the people in America identified as Christian; this number then dropped to just over 80 percent for the next two decades. Since the beginning of this century the number of people who self-identified as Christians declined 15 percent over the next 18 years to 67 percent.[9] This is almost a one percent drop per year. The major change is the great number of people who have changed from identifying with Christianity to those who do not identify with any religion. In 2015, an article in *Psychology Today* stated, "The ranks of the non-religious have grown by 19 million since 2007; there are now approximately 56 million Americans who do not identify with any religion, and these so-called 'nones' are now more numerous than Catholics or mainline Protestants."[10] America is not being overrun by religions from other cultures. One study showed that "Jewish, Buddhist, and Muslim teens remain small minorities in the United States (at 1.6 percent, 1.0 percent and 1.5 percent of 2015 10th graders, respectively)."[11]

---

9. http://news.gallup.com/poll/1690/religion.aspx.
10. Zuckerman, "Christianity Declining, Secularism Rising," para. 5.
11. Twenge, *iGen*, 120.

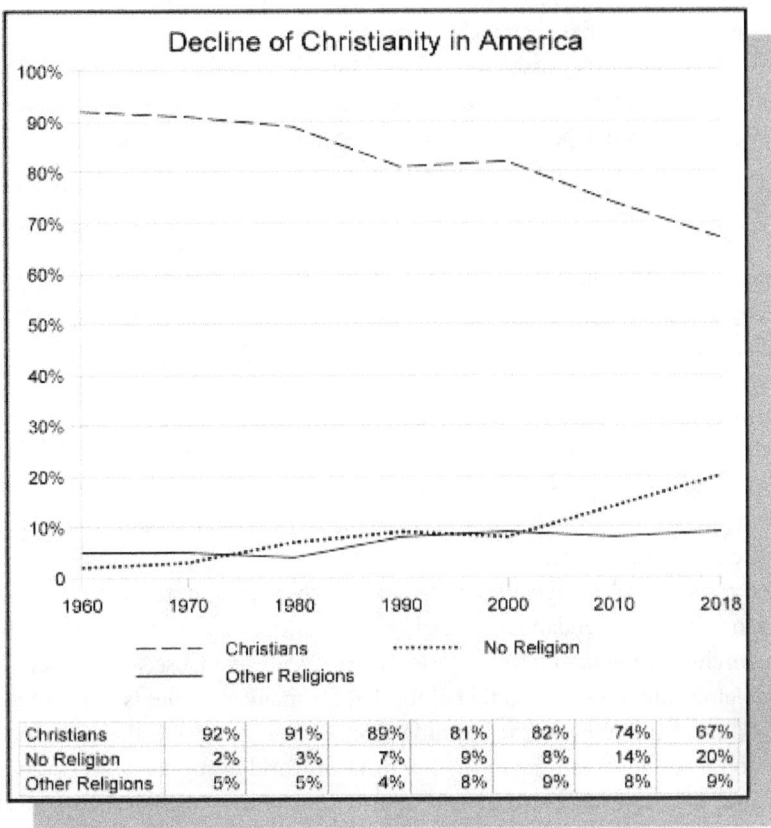

THE PROBLEM IN EUROPE

Europe is already far ahead of the United States in seeing the decline of Christianity. Ken Ham states: "A spiritual black plague has almost killed the next generation of European believers."[12] And Jean Twenge comments: "Even as churches in Europe have emptied, Americans have remained very religious in comparison. For a long time, scholars of American religion maintained that religious practice and belief were relatively stable in the United States."[13] The major differences between Europe and the United States is the wide range of denominations that has led to a competitive religious environment and aggressive conservative church movements. European churches are generally nominal, liberal state churches, and evangelical

12. Ham and Beemer, *Already Gone*, 22.
13. Twenge, *iGen*, 120.

denominations are relatively small in Europe as compared to the United States. The nominal, liberal churches of America have been losing membership similar to the losses in Europe. However, religion was not declining in the United States due to the rise of the evangelicals in the last half of the twentieth century. Now that the evangelical numbers have stopped growing in America, it has led to a decline in the last two decades similar to what has occurred in Europe.

The American heritage lies in the British Isles. Our concepts of government, the majority of settlers, and our religious heritage all came from England. England birthed groups such as the Quakers, the Puritans, the Baptists, and the Methodists, all of which exemplified the power of God and changed their culture. It was also in England that the great missions movement of our day began. Including the influence England has had on the United States as well as the rest of the world, Great Britain and its people may have had more positive impact for God than any other country in the last 1,000 years. Unfortunately, religious disaster has befallen England. According to statistics given in *Already Gone*, only 6.3 percent of the total population in England are regular churchgoers, and between 1998 and 2005, "church attendance dropped by an alarming 22 percent."[14] Some 1,500 churches in England have had their final service and closed their doors to religious life forever.[15] All that seems left for many churches is to read their obituary and bulldoze the buildings. Yet, only a little more than a century ago these churches were in the forefront of world evangelism; and even in the mid-twentieth century these places were alive, bustling, and packed with attendees. The world has watched "the plummeting spirituality of a nation that has lost its roots—its foundation. England, the country that was once a cornerstone of western Christianity, is now, by and large, a wasteland of lost souls."[16]

DECLINE IN AMERICAN CHURCHES

America is following the same negative trajectory. Unless there are major changes, the same statements will be made about our country in another generation. Within the last few decades, Christianity in America has veered off course and is headed for a horrific crash as has happened in Europe. "For every American who was raised without religion but has since joined a religious group as an adult, four Americans who were raised with religion have

---

14. Ham and Beemer, *Already Gone*, 12.
15. Ham and Beemer, *Already Gone*, 10.
16. Ham and Beemer, *Already Gone*, 11–12.

dropped out as adults; thus, secularism is clearly winning the joining/leaving game by a ratio of 4 to 1."[17] The American church must awaken while there is still time to reverse the consequences and undo the damage. "Where Europe is today spiritually America will be tomorrow—and for the same reasons, if the Church does not recognize where the foundational problem lies and address it."[18] It is easy to identify that there is a problem, but the real issue is: What can and must be done to avert the approaching disaster?

All church groups are not declining equally. Catholic churches and mainline churches are seeing the greatest decline.[19] Conservative evangelical churches are doing better, but all indications are that their decline is just beginning and will accelerate. The greatest declines came in mid-sized churches while at the same time the largest churches grew rapidly.[20] The success of megachurches has gained the most attention and has led to the false perception that the church is growing overall. It is projected if the current trends continue "in 2050, the percentage of the U.S. population attending church will be almost half of what it was in 1990."[21] When mainline denominational leaders were warned of the "emerging patterns of decline in attendance in the 1980s, they were largely in denial. . . . Now evangelical denominations are also beginning to experience decline. Twenty-three of twenty-five major evangelical denominations, including the Southern Baptist Convention, are experiencing declining attendance patterns. We are also losing 20- and 30-year-olds at a disturbing rate, a rate we have not seen before."[22]

The major cause for the decline in church attendance is a massive loss of young people who were raised in the church that no longer attend. "A mass exodus is underway. Most youth of today will not be coming to church tomorrow."[23] This decline of the church and the loss of many of the youth of the next generation should have been an obvious problem. According to Ken Ham, "Many of us saw it coming but didn't want to admit it. After all, our churches looked healthy on the surface. We saw bubbling Sunday schools and dynamic youth ministries."[24] "In separate studies Josh McDowell, LifeWay Research, the Barna Group, and secular researchers, including

17. Zuckerman, "Christianity Declining, Secularism Rising," para. 6.
18. Ham and Beemer, *Already Gone*, 26.
19. Bailey, "Christianity Faces Sharp Decline."
20. Olson, *American Church in Crisis*, 86.
21. "Startling Facts," the heading for sec. 7.
22. Sine, "Wakeup Call for Evangelicals," para. 2.
23. Ham and Beemer, *Already Gone*, 22.
24. Ham and Beemer, *Already Gone*, 22.

at UCLA, have all landed at figures between 69 and 80 percent of evangelicals in their twenties who leave the faith."[25] One study has tracked the religious involvement of teens since 1966 with over 11 million respondents. Their analysis reveals "a seismic generational shift in religious commitment. Twice as many high school seniors, and 3 times as many college students, described their religion as 'none' in the 2010s (vs. the early 1980s)."[26] This study also showed that about 68 percent of college students affiliated with a religion compared to 83 percent of their parents at the time when they went to college[27] (see chart). "Millennials are the least religious generation in the last six decades.

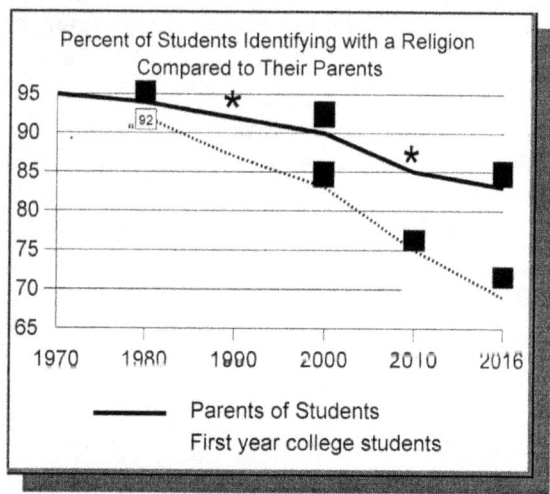

If we assume Americans in the 1950s and earlier were just as religious as those in the 1970s, millennials are the least religious generation in American history."[28] This is also true of young adults when they begin raising families. Some parents do return for the sake of having their children raised in church; however, in spite of this, "the decline in attending religious services for this group in their prime family-building years has been just as steep as that for young adults."[29] Of those who leave the church, "35 percent

25. Dickerson, *Great Evangelical Recession*, 98–99.
26. Twenge, "Our Changing Culture," para. 5.
27. Twenge, *iGen*, 122.
28. Twenge, "Our Changing Culture," para. 8.
29. Twenge, *iGen*, 124.

of prodigals find their way back into evangelical church attendance, while 65 percent do not."[30]

God will move on to other countries and other people in the working out of his great salvation. We will become just like the Jewish nation which rejected Christ and were cut out of the spiritual olive tree. God simply moved on to the gentiles. Tragically, we who have been given the greatest religious heritage since the Jews of Christ's day are walking in their same footsteps. Unless America is renewed, God will simply move on. I pray God will give us one more chance and revive us once again. I want to be part of that revival.

---

30. Dickerson, *Great Evangelical Recession*, 101.

CHAPTER 2

Denominational Difficulty

The best way to describe the difficulty which the evangelical church world faces is to study the denominational growth rates for various groups within the evangelical movement. The Southern Baptist Church, which is the largest Protestant denomination in the United States, is the best representative of those with a Baptist background. The Holiness movement best represents the evangelical element of Methodism. The Church of the Nazarene and the Wesleyan Church comprise a majority of those who identify with the Holiness movement. The Pentecostal groups which rose from a division in the Holiness movement in the first decade of the twentieth century are represented by two of the largest groups, The Assemblies of God and the Church of God (Cleveland, TN). Several denominations which are on the fringes of Christian orthodoxy but are emphatic about their doctrine are still growing. The Seventh-day Adventist Church is the representative of this group.

Conservative denominations in America were seeing phenomenal growth at the mid-point of the last century. Yet, there has been a consistent decline in the rate of growth over the last fifty years in almost all of those organizations. Numbers have now flattened; and unless radical changes are made, many of these groups will face collapse. The same trends are occurring across a broad range of theological perspectives, but not among radical groups outside of the evangelical mainstream. These plummeting growth rates are copying what happened to mainline denominations in the mid-twentieth century. The following three charts show the negative trajectory in which evangelical church denominations now find themselves.

Dominating the evangelical Protestant church world is the Southern Baptist Church. Growing from about 5 million in 1940, it became the largest Protestant denomination in the United States by 1970. However, after peaking at more than 16 million in 2003, its growth flattened and then began a slow decline.[1] Whatever happens to the Southern Baptists will have a major impact upon all the conservative churches in America. As a denomination it is a mix between evangelicals and a more liberal belief system.

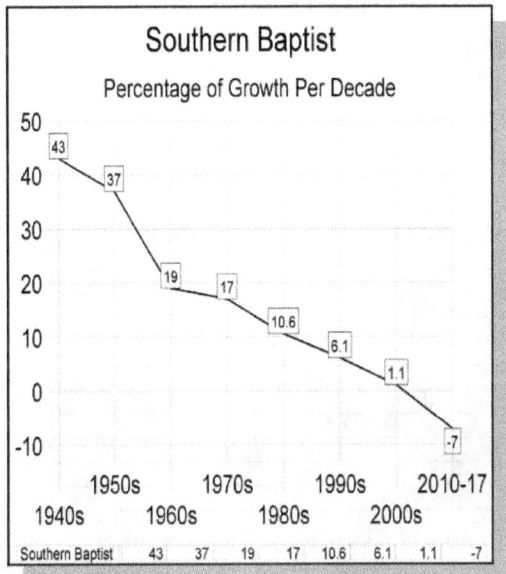

What has happened to the Holiness movement? In its glory days it believed it was going to take the world for the doctrine of holiness. From almost nothing it exploded across the country within a few decades. Then

1. **Southern Baptist Data**

Year	Churches	Membership	percent growth over previous decade
1940	25,018	4,949,174	
1950	27,788	7,079,889	43 percent
1960	32,251	9,731,591	37 percent
1970	34,340	11,628,032	19 percent
1980	35,778	13,600,126	17 percent
1990	37,922	15,038,409	10.6 percent
2000	41,588	15,960,308	6.1 percent
2010	45,727	16,136,044	1.1 percent
2017	47,544	15,005,638	-7 percent

http://www.thearda.com/Denoms/D_1087.asp. For the 2017 statistics, see http://www.sbc.net/fastfacts/.

its rate of growth began to decline and today is now numerically declining in America. The movement has lost the ability to start more churches than are being closed. Consistently, the Holiness movement's growth rates have dropped almost every decade. From doubling each decade for the first several decades, its growth rate percentages dropped to the 30 percent range by mid-century. These percentages continued to decline into the twenties and were about 10 percent by the turn of the millennium. But far more seriously, actual numbers peaked and began to drop.[2]

2. Church of the Nazarene Data

Year	Churches	Members	percent growth over previous decade
1929	1,774	77,662	
1940	2,612	165,532	113
1950	3,480	226,684	37
1960	4,458	307,629	36
1970	4,636	383,284	25
1980	4,853	484,276	26
1990	*5165	567543*	17
2000	5,070	636,564	12
2010	5,058	649,836	2.0
2018	5,172	628,339	-3.0

*These are an average of 1989 and 1991 since the statistics were not given for 1990.
http://www.thearda.com/Denoms/D_1441.asp. For the 2017 statistics, see https://www.nazarene.org/sites/default/files/docs/GenSec/Statistics/Annual percent20Church percent20Statistical percent20Reports percent202018.pdf.

Wesleyan Church Data

Year	Churches	Members	percent growth over previous decade
1929	1059	37,980	
1940	1438	51,604*	32
1950	2036	63,471*	27
1960	2,081	76,544	21
1970	1,898	84,499	10
1980	1,710	108,273	28
1990	1,628	115,474	6.7
2000	1,602	128,971	11.7
2010	1,715	139,330	8.5
2018	1,557	138,190	-0.8

*Before 1970, the numbers are a compilation of Pilgrim Holiness and Wesleyan Methodist numbers. 1951 statistics were used for Pilgrim Holiness and 1942 for Wesleyan Methodist since these were the numbers reported.

Black and Drury, *Story of the Wesleyan Church*, 283–84. Statistics for 2018, see https://www.wesleyan.org/?s=Statistics.

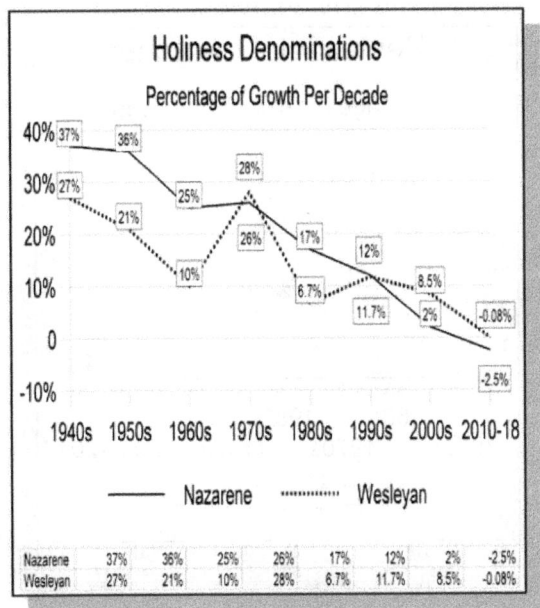

It is clear something has gone wrong; yet growth has been a major theme of these movements for several decades. It seems the harder the leaders have tried to overcome the inertia, the worse it has become. It is imperative that answers are found. The movement still has a message the world needs—the pursuit of holiness. As is true in many other groups, the problem is predominantly a difficulty for the United States. Most denominations in the Holiness movement are on the march forward overseas and have more foreign churches than are located in this country. Worldwide they are still growing rapidly.

Pentecostal churches have had perhaps the greatest growth rates across the last century. The Pentecostal doctrine has risen to become one of the major belief systems in the country. However, their growth rates have plummeted about as much as have the growth rates of other groups.

Overall they are not yet shrinking in the number of members. In the decline of growth these churches may be only one decade behind other denominations if current trends continue. The Assemblies of God has seen a major drop in growth.[3]

Data after 2010 was not available for the Church of God (Cleveland, TN); however, the statistics available from 2006 through 2010 show a major drop in the growth of the movement. These five years only show a growth of 3.9 percent, with most of this occurring in 2006 and 2007. Likewise the total number of churches that are part of the Church of God (Cleveland, TN) declined between 2006 and 2010.[4]

3. **Assemblies of God Data**

Year	Churches	Members	percent growth over previous decade
1940	3,930	198,834	
1950	5,950	318,478	60 percent
1960	8,233	508,602	60 percent
1970	8,619	645891	27 percent
1980	9,773	1064490	65 percent
1990	11,353	1298,191	22 percent
2000	12,084	1,506,834	16 percent
2010	12,457	1,753,881	16 percent
2017	13,004	1,853,273	5.7 percent

https://ag.org/About/Statistics. See the full report for 2017 in website article.

4. **Church of God Cleveland Membership Data**

UNORTHODOX CHRISTIAN DENOMINATIONS

For those who hold orthodox Christian doctrines, it is uncomfortable to note that some of the fastest-growing groups are outside traditional Christian beliefs. Some that are doing quite well in denominational growth do not accept orthodox doctrines about the Trinity, teachings about an eternal hell, or the deity of Christ. The most recent available numbers for the Jehovah's Witnesses were 19 percent for the decade from 2000 to 2010.[5] The United Pentecostal Church, which still has strict dress standards but does not believe in the Trinity, is showing rapid growth; but membership numbers were not available for the last decade.[6] The Church of Jesus Christ of Latter-day Saints, commonly known as the Mormons, was still having growth rates of about 20 percent as of 2010, gaining almost 1 million adherents during the first decade of the 21st century.[7]

The Seventh-day Adventist Church is still showing rapid growth. Their growth has dropped from gains in the 30 percent range to the low twenties. Their growth rates, while quite rapid, have not historically been as high as some others; but their growth rates have only slightly declined. They have shown a growth rate in the 20 percent range for four decades. The last set of numbers covers only seven years, which would make the growth percentage for the decade at 26 percent if it continued at the same rate.[8]

Year	Churches	Members	percent growth over previous decade
1940	1,602	63,216	
1950	3,368	121,706	93 percent
1960	3,280	170,261	40 percent
1970	4,024	272,276	60 percent
1980	5,176	435,012	60 percent
1990	5,841	620,393	43 percent
2000	6,426	895,536	44 percent
2006	6,569	1,032,550	13 percent
2010	6,481	1,074,047	3.9 percent

http://www.thearda.com/Denoms/D_1347.asp.

5. http://www.thearda.com/Denoms/D_1107.asp.
6. http://www.thearda.com/Denoms/D_1016.asp.
7. http://www.thearda.com/Denoms/D_1117.asp.
8. **Seventh-day Adventists Data**

Year	Churches	Members	Growth Rate
1929	2,250	119,843	
1940	2,565	176,218	47 percent
1950	2,712	237,168	35 percent
1960	3,032	317,852	34 percent
1970	3,218	420,419	32 percent
1980	3,730	571,141	36 percent
1990	4,217	717,466	26 percent
2000	4,486	880,921	23 percent
2010	4,916	1,060,386	20 percent
2017		1,249,715*	18 percent

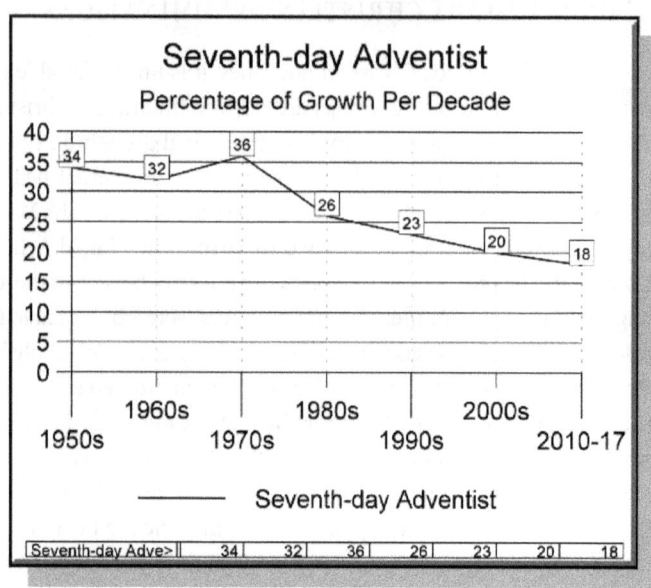

The more radical religious groups are doing better than are other denominations. Seventh-day Adventists are dogmatic about Saturday worship as a necessity for entrance to heaven and have other very restrictive behaviors such as not allowing meat to be eaten. Likewise, the other groups which are seeing rapid growth are also dogmatic about their beliefs, evangelistically focused, and very restrictive about behavior. It certainly seems there is a strong tie between demanding a strict lifestyle and denominational growth.

The modern mindset of church growth has focused upon using modern marketing principles to successfully build a church along with teaching effective leadership skills. Most of these principles from the church growth movement have been very valuable and effective. This emphasis has produced wildly successful churches in the short term. The problem is that often the necessary theological foundations that produce lasting converts who are totally dedicated to God have been left out. It takes time and effort to build upon a lasting foundation. Churches built to a great degree upon the personality and ability of the pastor and upon pleasing the people have little stability. Megachurches of this type can collapse as quickly as they are birthed; all it takes is for a storm to strike. With weak doctrinal foundations and little commitment, the people scatter. Often the crowds have come for the music and entertainment but will not stay through the problems. It also seems impossible to replicate megachurch successes across entire

http://www.thearda.com/Denoms/D_1108.asp.

denominations. Other less dynamic pastors who are in areas with lesser possibilities cannot achieve what the superstars have accomplished. In addition, pastors who demand change in a person's life often find the modern concept of growth undermines their own efforts in outreach. Along with the spectacular successes, the church world needs to once again see the average church with the average pastor consistently and effectually evangelize.

In America, the church has experienced one of the greatest success stories in world history. Our country has gone from revival to revival, and "the master trend of American religious history is a long, slow, and consistent increase in religious participation."[9] Unfortunately, the evangelistic strength of the church overall is gone, and the American church is currently in decline. Yes, there are a number of notable, high-profile success stories; but these gains are not sufficient to counteract the losses. Perhaps Ken Ham put it best when he said, "We are one generation away from the evaporation of church as we know it. Slowly but certainly the church of the future is headed toward the morgue and will continue to do so—unless we come to better understand what is happening and implement a clear, biblical plan to circumvent it."[10]

---

9. Finke and Stark, *Churching of America, 1776–1990*, 274.
10. Ham and Beemer, *Already Gone*, 25.

CHAPTER 3

Contrasting the Models of Church Growth

Historically, church growth has occurred through what could be called a conversion model of church growth. This methodology focused upon exposing an individual's spiritual need and challenging him or her to make a radical change. This methodology was confrontational, theologically focused, and demanded repentance and a change both in beliefs and in lifestyle. Many of those confronted rejected the admonitions, never came to church, or quit attending. There were some, though, who repented, were converted, and then became fervent members of the church. Growth occurred as these new people became part of the church. Revival meetings with professional revivalists were often used to bring outsiders into the church for conversion. Sunday schools reached out to the children in the community and, likewise, exposed children who were formerly not part of the church to the gospel message. Often this provided a link to the family for evangelism. Society has changed, and rarely do revival services attract the community as they once did. Children's ministries do still have some success, but other options of entertainment have limited its former appeal. Cultural changes do mean that efforts that have worked in the past may not be effective today, and the church must adapt to discover other methods which do work, but which do not undermine the foundation of the church.

Studies in sociology have proven that denominations which grow are strict. According to Dean Kelley in *Why Conservative Churches Are Growing*, "Strong organizations tend to increase in membership and weak ones to diminish. . . . [and] strong organizations are strict."[1] The key component for measuring the strength of an organization is whether it is attracting or losing members. This concept also holds true for many other social organizations that are not religious. Religious groups which are outside orthodox Christianity also grow and thrive by conversion methodology. Sometimes short-term success can be obtained by compromising the principles of a group, but organizations that thrive long term do not compromise their values for a less offensive approach. Instead, successful groups have always worked to convince the culture around them of the validity of their belief system. This was the method followed by Christ and the early church. In America's heritage, Methodists were known to be aggressive and outspoken in their doctrine and evangelism. They preached a hellfire-and-brimstone message to the sinners of their day, "and stressed spiritual conversion and a strong individual responsibility to God. . . . Their message seldom excluded the topics of sin and salvation, or hellfire and redemption."[2]

THE CULTURAL ACCOMMODATION MODEL

The new, modern evangelical model of evangelism could be called the seeker-sensitive or the cultural-accommodation model. This is the concept that has been promoted by the Church Growth movement. Perhaps the best known advocate of these concepts is Rick Warren. His book, *The Purpose Driven Church*, became one of the top bestsellers and is one of the most influential books in the religious world. "More than 320,000 pastors and church leaders from over 120 countries have attended Purpose-Driven Church seminars in eighteen languages, and tens of thousands of churches have adopted the PDC [Purpose-Driven Church] strategy."[3] This seeker-sensitive concept is geared to attracting new people from the world:

> Therefore, the services must be designed in such a way that [the attendee] he will be comfortable, entertained . . . that the ministry of the church must be stylized after those things to which the unsaved are accustomed . . . [including] the language used, the music performed, the casual attire worn or even the message proclaimed from the pulpit. The character, the style and the contemporary interests of the unregenerate community are

---

1. Kelley, *Why Conservative Churches Are Growing*, 95.
2. Finke and Stark, *Churching of America, 1776–1990*, 85.
3. Blanchard and Lucarini, *Can We Rock the Gospel?*, 28.

what determines the makeup, the appearance and the content of the weekend services.[4]

Rick Warren has personally been spectactularly successful. He started and built his own church, Saddleback Community Church, into a congregation which has one of the largest attendances in the United States. The "Purpose-Driven Church" model has been followed by thousands of others, many of whom have successfully built large congregations. In the minds of many if not most evangelicals, this has become the only successful model of church growth which is working in our culture today. In his seminar, "Rick Warren made it expressly known that if one wants growth, dynamic growth, then he must do it this 'Saddleback' way, but if that person decides to stay in the conservative, traditional mode, his ministry and church will wither on the vine."[5] Many churches in America have plunged headlong into this concept. Traditional music has been abandoned. The minister now dresses in a casual way and wears a hairstyle that relates to those of the world.

Holiness churches have not been exempt. If this was the new way to evangelize, they wanted to be part of what was happening. "Evangelism has always been a twin passion with holiness. So, many holiness churches—at least the growing ones—suppressed their natural reticence and adopted church-growth thinking in a wholesale way."[6] "The possibility of dynamic growth for struggling churches, especially old-fashioned, Bible-believing, Bible-preaching, fundamental churches, is tremendously appealing."[7] Even those who are not willing to go completely into the new methodology have accepted much of the thinking of the Church Growth movement. Anyone who disagrees with the concepts of the cultural accommodation model espoused by the Purpose-Driven Church and Church Growth movements must effectively explain why it is successful in many instances.

PROBLEMS OF THE CULTURAL ACCOMMODATION MODEL

The rise of numbers of megachurches in our country, especially among evangelical churches, gives the impression of growth. Most of the focus has always been upon the successful churches rather than looking at the big picture. It is easy to overlook the fact that smaller churches are not doing well. Most pastors and church leaders have been attempting to emulate the

---

4. Cloud, "Church Growth Movement," 10.
5. Cloud, "Church Growth Movement," 7.
6. Drury et al., *Counterpoint*, 22.
7. Cloud, "Church Growth Movement," 1.

success they have seen in the larger congregations, yet with little success. In fact, as evangelical churches have plunged into the Church Growth movement wholeheartedly, the growth rate of evangelical churches has collapsed. For example, the Southern Baptist Church, which is Rick Warren's own denomination, stopped growing about ten years after the publication of Warren's book. The church had grown 130 percent between 1950 and 2005.[8] Today, the denomination is shrinking, and the Southern Baptists have lost more than a million members since the church peaked in 2006.[9] Holiness denominations are facing the same problem. The Church of the Nazarene, the Wesleyan Church, the Free Methodist Church, and the Salvation Army have all flatlined in membership growth in America.[10] Often the growth that is occurring, especially for the Wesleyans, is highly concentrated in the largest churches in the denomination.[11]

What may be occurring is the same trend which is occurring in American business. When a discount store such as Walmart arrives in a small town, it does not increase the overall consumption of goods purchased by the community. It merely transfers their purchases to a larger, more convenient store. Before long, Main Street may be filled with boarded-up windows from the stores which have closed their doors. John Dickerson, in *The Great Evangelical Recession*, noted that "more than half of evangelicals now attend these larger growing churches, which continue to absorb folks from smaller churches. As a result, most of us have the perception that the church is growing."[12] Unfortunately, evangelical attendance in the United States in most states is now in decline. The trend from 2000 to 2005 shows "a decrease in attendance at evangelical churches, even as the population grew in almost all those states."[13]

While megachurches are doing well in attendance, smaller churches are struggling. Successful growth for many large churches has come by having a dynamic pastor, a wide range of programs, adequate buildings, and an atmosphere in which any evangelical would be comfortable. Doctrinal differences and demands regarding Christian behavior are downplayed. Smaller churches without the necessary infrastructure or dynamic ministry try to replicate the success of the larger church. As small churches de-emphasize

---

8. hirr.hartsem.edu/research/fastfacts/fast_facts.html.

9. Stetzer, "Southern Baptist Decline Continues." The SBC actually had its highest peak in 2003 then dropped slightly and peaked again in 2006.

10. http://www.thearda.com/Denoms/.

11. Black and Drury, *Story of the Wesleyan Church*, 290–91.

12. Dickerson, *Great Evangelical Recession*, 117.

13. Dickerson, *Great Evangelical Recession*, 118.

doctrine and behavioral guidelines for the sake of growth, it undermines the very reason why those churches exist. Many of the congregation, especially the young people, loosed from their doctrinal moorings, depart for the local megachurch of another belief system. Most communities already have successful large-church ministries, and if being like the megachurch is the goal, people in smaller churches question why their church should exist. Why not just close the church doors and attend elsewhere? The very thing that brings numerical success in the large church ultimately destroys the smaller church and eventually the denomination. The conversion model, which emphasized the reason for existence, is what has enabled churches with a distinctive doctrinal belief, such as Holiness churches, to be planted and to thrive throughout our country.

It has become increasingly difficult to convert new people and to establish new churches. Now evangelical churches and most Holiness denominations "are not converting and cannot convert non-Christian adult Americans, especially native-born white people, in significant numbers."[14] Most of the people who are unchurched already profess to be a Christian. They may not attend church and may live a lifestyle of rebellion against God, but the modern eternal security belief has convinced them heaven is already guaranteed. This has undermined their need for church. If they do come, they only come if they feel like it. Commitment is gone. Sunday school attendance is shrinking rapidly, and few even bother to come for Sunday evening service. Mid-week prayer meetings or Bible studies have become a thing of the past in many places. According to Ken Ham, "Church leaders today seem to think that programs, entertainment, music, and many other things are what is needed to reach people and keep them in church . . . Our research showed something very different—that people want good Bible teaching."[15] Moral behavior in the church has crumbled to the point that the lives of the church people effectively mirror that of the world. The modern Church Growth movement, with its effort to avoid controversy, is, to a great degree, responsible for the shallowness of the church today.

The shallowness of the modern megachurch methodology has led to the loss of fervency for deep spirituality among Holiness proponents. Prayer was a major key to rapid growth in the early days of the Holiness movement. C. Helen Mooshian, an early Nazarene, tells about a group of people who prayed all night every Saturday night for several years.[16] This fervency was also evident in church services. Because of their excited worship services,

---

14. Dickerson, *Great Evangelical Recession*, 118.
15. Ham and Beemer, *Already Gone*, 113.
16. Mooshian, *His Ambassador*, 26.

Nazarenes were known as "Noise-arenes" in some places. Too often the same excitement and presence of God are missing in the church services, revivals, and camp meetings of today. During these movings of the Spirit, altars were commonly lined with seekers who were converted. Currently, lasting conversions of nonchurched people who become committed to the old-fashioned way are becoming rare where they were once commonplace.

When people are no longer attracted because God is moving, it will not be long until entertainment or another substitute will replace the power of God. Ken Ham noted the common belief, saying,

> We think that if we can make it [the church] dynamic, energetic, and fit the style of the generation we're trying to reach, the epidemic will be stopped and young people will start flooding back into the Church. That's simply not the case. Our research showed that music is not a fundamental factor in young adults choosing to leave or stay at a church—but the preaching of God's word is.[17]

When the exposition of Scripture and the moving of the presence of God in the transformation of lives is not present, people will always look for a substitute to attract the crowds. Often people turn to better leadership skills, more dynamic and exciting services, entertainment, social activities, fellowship, better buildings, etc. Many of these ideas are excellent and are desperately needed, but they do not address the core problem. Some leaders have been capable in a worldly way of using modern methodology and marketing skills to build a large congregation. The problem is not the effectiveness of these ideas, but rather that, if the true purpose of the church has eroded away, the church will eventually crumble. There is no substitute for a deep underlying, complete, personal commitment to Jesus Christ. Churches must lay the correct foundation first and then build upon that, using all the available skills in our world to build Christ's church.

> There is no substitute for a deep underlying, complete, personal commitment to Jesus Christ

Another serious problem of the culturally sensitive growth model is the impact it is having upon young people and children born and raised in the church. Our churches should grow if we merely saved our own children. It is thought that one of the major factors in the growth of the early church was a higher fertility rate among Christians who then passed on their

---

17. Ham and Beemer, *Already Gone*, 110.

beliefs to their children.[18] This is also true of other religions, and population growth among Muslims is the major growth factor for that religion today. In contrast, the modern concepts of church growth strike a dagger in the heart of converting the next generation. Children are reared with modern preaching and teaching that rarely emphasizes doctrinal beliefs; and when they are taught, often unpopular doctrines are presented as almost optional. America is currently raising a generation of young people who no longer believe in the faith of their parents. Studies show "About 70 percent of . . . church attendees from the millennial generation quit attending church by age 23."[19] "Two out of three of these never return."[20] The loyal core of any local church, both in its commitment to that local church, the denomination, and its theological grid, should be those who were born and reared in that congregation. If that core is undermined for the sake of temporary growth, is there really any long-lasting future?

Another major problem with the cultural-accommodation model of church growth is that it is unscriptural. The gospel still demands one's all. Christ stated, "If any man will come after me, let him deny himself, and take up his cross, and follow me" (Matt 16:24). Jesus himself confronted the rich young ruler with the very words which drove him away (Matt 19:16–22). In order not to lose those whom we are passionately trying to reach, the church has often tried to strip out the cost. Often it is not just a poor attitude or approach by church members that is the problem, it is that the cost of Christianity is truly understood and rejected. When a person leaves, often he will go to a church which does not demand a high level of consecration. It is then thought that if only a better approach had been used, he would not have left. In reality, a person who comes face-to-face with the cost of the gospel and is not willing to commit himself to Christ will leave eventually. Conversion evangelism demands the same challenge that Christ gave the rich young ruler. Christ demanded a person's entire commitment. The result will be the same today. Many will walk away from the church and reject Christ. The church has always been disturbed by those who are offended by the message of the gospel and leave. The church's purpose is to be a soul-saving station, and failure to touch a person for Christ is unacceptable; but ultimately he or she must choose Christ individually.

---

18. Stark, *Rise of Christianity*, 128.
19. Dickerson, *Great Evangelical Recession*, 99.
20. Dickerson, *Great Evangelical Recession*, 101.

CHAPTER 4

Necessity of the Power of God

The city had been completely transformed. People abandoned their worldly books and began reading sermons: "all prayed, went to church and the rich gave freely to the poor."[1] Even street gangs began singing hymns. Culminating the great revival, children went down the street collecting all sorts of materials which the city of that day considered worldly or obscene. This was gathered together in a huge pile in the public square. The stack of items to be burned towered 60 feet high and was 240 feet in circumference. "People surrounded it holding hands and singing hymns while church bells tolled, and it was burned."[2] Florence, Italy in 1497 experienced revival like few other cities have ever experienced. What was the secret? It was because of the power of the Spirit of God.

    Leading the revival was a monk, Girolamo Savonarola. He was deeply pious and quite disturbed about the immorality and wickedness of his day. The Catholic Church just before Martin Luther was at one of its lowest points morally. The evil of that time was perhaps as bad if not worse than our day. Furthermore, the people did not even have the Bible in their common language and knew nothing of salvation by faith. Yet, in the utter darkness of that time lived Savonarola, who was known for his fasting and prayer to God for the people in the city around him. Savonarola's preaching, however, had little impact. He spoke in Florence in a small chapel while the crowds flocked to hear a popular preacher who never denounced the evils of the day.

1. Lawson, *Deeper Experiences of Famous Christians*, 77.
2. Duewel, *Heroes of the Holy Life*, 152.

One day all of that changed; Savonarola had a special encounter with God and received a new power. Now when he thundered out the denunciation of their sins, the people of Florence were held spellbound. Thousands of souls were convicted by the power of God, began to agonize over their sins, and the sound of weeping permeated the services. Now instead of the little crowds, he spoke in the largest cathedral to a packed building of 15,000 in attendance. Many came hours before the doors opened just to find a place to sit.[3] The difference was not really the message, the minister, or the town; it was the empowering of the Holy Spirit.

STATEMENTS OF CHRIST

Before Christ left, he instructed his disciples to "tarry ye in the city of Jerusalem, until ye be endued with power from on high" (Luke 24:49). After receiving this power, the disciples converted 3,000 on the day of Pentecost. The power of God permeated the ministry of the apostles. The city of Jerusalem was changed, and the power then began to spread throughout the known world of that day. The apostle Paul stated, "Our gospel came not unto you in word only, but also in power, and in the Holy Ghost" (1 Thess 1:5). It is no wonder the opponents of the gospel accused Paul of having "turned the world upside down" (Acts 17:6).

The same power that drove the church forward during the days of the apostles has been repeated down throughout history. Men such as Martin Luther, John Knox, John Wesley, George Whitefield, Charles Finney, and a multitude of others preached with such power that the countries in which they lived were never the same. In many instances they changed their culture from a godless, immoral community to one that lived righteously and worshiped God. No other country has been as blessed as has the United States. The First and Second Great Awakenings established America on a solid Christian foundation. From our beginnings revival has repeatedly swept across our country. In every one of these instances it has always been the power of the Holy Spirit working through Spirit-filled men. Their preaching was always powerful and bold, but also convicting.

Tragically it seems that power is gone. Yes, there are times in which there is a measure of the moving of God, but not the culture- and community-changing power of the past. It seems the church lies helpless before the allure of the world. The world is changing the church rather than the church impacting the world. Growth methodology no longer relies upon the power of God but upon programs that please people. Yet in spite of all our efforts,

---

3. Duewel, *Heroes of the Holy Life*, 152.

it seems that little long-term success is occurring. It is time to face reality: unless God moves, our churches will die.

Jesus told his disciples that "without me ye can do nothing" (John 15:5). A church without God will be powerless and, in reality, cause damage to the kingdom of God and the souls of people. There will be many people who believe they are right with God, but because of being deceived by their church, they will not make it into heaven. In Matthew 7:13–14, Jesus teaches that in life there are two roads which people take: a broad way and a narrow way. The broad way leads to destruction but contains most of the people. This would include many religious people who feel they are going to heaven, but in reality they are badly deceived. There is no greater tragedy than for a person to unwittingly go to hell by way of the church. Religious deception has been one of Satan's greatest tools throughout history.

A church may do everything right, but if it does not have the power of Christ in it, no good will be accomplished. The doctrine may be correct, but if there is no power of God the church will turn people away from the truth. The Bible says, "The letter killeth, but the Spirit giveth life" (2 Cor 3:6). Even churches that work hard at the job of reaching people and standing for truth have still failed. They would be like the church of Ephesus in the book of Revelation. The church had done everything right but had left its first love. Jesus informed them that unless they repented, he would come and remove their candlestick out of its place. The priority is not to have more evangelistic programs, but to first obtain more of God. Tarrying in prayer before God until a person is filled with the Spirit of God is an absolute necessity for the survival and progress of the church.

KEYS OF REVIVAL

Beginning in 1949, Duncan Campbell was involved in a mighty revival that shook the Isle of Lewis in the Hebrides Islands. Before the revival, true religion seemed to be disappearing from the island. There was a "terrible drift away from the ordinances of the church, especially by the young people of the island, and the dearth of conversions in their congregations."[4] The young people of the island had abandoned the church and were involved in all manner of wickedness. It seemed many of the churches would soon close. Then revival changed everything. Campbell stated,

> The power of God swept into the parish. And an awareness of God gripped the community such as hadn't been known for over

---

4. http://www.calltoprayer.org.uk/encourager37.htm.

100 years.... the following day, the looms were silent, little work was done on the farms as men and women gave themselves to thinking on eternal things gripped by eternal realities.[5]

God moved for almost three years, and his power swept throughout the island. "The whole region seemed saturated with God. Wherever people were—in their homes, fields, on the road—they were awesomely aware of God's presence."[6]

Intercessory prayer was one of the keys to this outpouring of God. It began with two old ladies in their eighties, Peggy and Christine Smith, who began to plead with God for revival. For months they pled with God for revival, praying over each person who lived in each house in the village. In another place seven men met to pray for an extended time two or three times a week. This continued for about a month and a half; and then while they were pleading the promises of God, one of the deacons stated, "It seems to me to be so much humbug to be praying as we are praying, to be waiting as we are waiting, if we ourselves are not rightly related to God."[7] Then he lifted his hands toward heaven and cried out, "Oh God! Are my hands clean? Is my heart pure?"[8] He then fell on the floor in a trance, and the presence of God swept into the barn in which they were praying. Soon they called an evangelist, Duncan Campbell; but God was already moving, and the revival was on even before he arrived.

Revival always brings new life to dying churches. No question but what revival transformed the churches in the Hebrides Islands. It filled the churches and changed the lives of sinful people, bringing them into a right relationship with God. It has always been this way. The Great Awakening in America converted tens of thousands of people and filled the churches. It laid the foundation for Christian heritage in our country. The Second Great Awakening continued the march of Christianity across the frontier and continued to convert the sinner and fill America's churches. During the Second Great Awakening the Baptist churches and the Methodist church became the dominant revivalistic institutions in our country. These awakenings in America, along with revival in England, also propelled the missionary zeal that has gone worldwide and is remaking the world. The terrible tragedy is that now Christianity is dying in the West. A Third Great Awakening is our only hope. All of our efforts to build the church and grow without God have been failures. In some instances churches have been filled with dead,

---

5. http://www.calltoprayer.org.uk/encourager37.htm, para. 15.
6. Duewel, *Revival Fire*, 309.
7. http://www.calltoprayer.org.uk/encourager37.htm, para. 14.
8. Duewel, *Revival Fire*, 307.

worldly, powerless, semi-pagan Christians. This is not Christianity, nor what God wants. In America today, the church has no power to overcome the world, sin, or Satan. Christianity has become a poor caricature of the real. Without genuine revival, Christianity in America is doomed.

> The church has no power to overcome the world, sin, or Satan. Christianity has become a poor caricature of the real.

Another key to revival is when the ministry denounces sin and the church repents. This was a characteristic of the Great Awakening in the eighteenth-century American colonies. The awakening began first under the ministry of Theodore Frelinghuysen, among the Dutch Reformed churches in central New Jersey. In his very first sermon upon arrival in his parish he appealed to the people to "lay aside all pride, haughtiness, and . . . humble themselves before the Lord."[9] To his complacent congregations Frelinghuysen "declared that people seeking eternal life must first undergo an agonizing conviction of their sinful condition. Such people are lost and damned while still in their natural state."[10] Gilbert Tennent and George Whitefield likewise denounced the sin of their day. Whitefield laid the blame clearly on the clergy, saying, "The reason why congregations have been so dead is because they had dead men preaching to them. How can dead men beget living children?"[11]

The keys to renewal in our church are the same as they have always been. Second Chronicles 7:14 says, "If my people, which are called by my name, shall humble themselves, and pray, and seek my face, and turn from their wicked ways; then will I hear from heaven, and will forgive their sin, and will heal their land." This biblical formula has never changed. The people in the church today need to humble themselves, repent of their sin, quit their wickedness, and seek the face of God until revival comes.

HOPE FOR THE FUTURE

It is the passionate cry of my heart for the fire of God to once again fall on our churches. The presence of God and his glory is the only answer to our needs. Our young people deserve and desperately need to see the outpouring of God as in the past. It is only the glory that will keep our people on

---

9. Sweet, *Revivalism in America*, 46.
10. Hardman, *Seasons of Refreshing*, 53.
11. Marshall and Manuel, *Light and the Glory*, 249.

the old-fashioned way. The world is going to hell on our very doorsteps, and all we can offer so often is a form of godliness, but no power to meet the needs. When Christ said, "Without me ye can do nothing" (John 15:5), he meant we are absolutely incapable of doing anything without his help. Nothing does mean nothing; yet we work tirelessly and continue failing. In every instance it is God's presence that is the answer. As Paul said, "I can do all things through Christ which strengtheneth me" (Phil 4:13). The choice is between doing nothing in our own strength or doing all things through Christ.

I am convinced revival will come, and America will have another spiritual awakening. It may take persecution, war, or economic collapse; but God will do whatever it takes to bring our country back to its knees. I pray it does not take these difficulties, but an understanding of how God dealt with Israel in the Old Testament clearly teaches he will do whatever it takes.

A number of years ago I was traveling with a school group when the vehicle ran out of gas. I was in charge and assumed the school had taken care of filling the bus with fuel. The bus driver paid no attention until the gas tank said empty. About 10:00 at night we found the engine sputtering, and then the bus rolled to a halt on a fairly empty highway about three miles from Vinita, Oklahoma. In order to get the bus to a safe place, I told about fifteen young men to push the bus ahead to a place off the road. It rolled easily; we could have pushed it to a gas station in a couple of hours as long as there were no hills. Thankfully, someone stopped and took me into town for gas. Soon we were back traveling on the power of the motor. Just as a bus is not meant to travel by means of being pushed, the church is not meant to move forward under human power; yet it seems we are exhausting ourselves pushing the church forward through our own strength. The Spirit of God is the engine for the church. The motor needs to be fueled, started, and put in gear. Our job is not to provide the power, but to harness the strength of the Spirit. We must allow the presence of God to flow through us to the church and the needs of people. It is only then that souls are truly transformed, and the church sees true lasting growth.

A CALL TO THE HOLINESS PEOPLE

It is a proven fact that a denomination must either have a revival or it will begin a process of collapse in about fifty years. The Holiness movement is now past that milestone. We are facing a desperate need for revival, or we will be faced with the only other alternative: ruin. Unfortunately for many, there is a smug certainty that our group will be the exception and defy history; yet, unless we have a revival, the wreckage of our denominations will soon be casualties just like other fallen groups in history. It is necessary to openly admit our need and cry out to God for help.

One serious crisis our group is facing is the inability to establish our own people in the faith. Many of our young people are abandoning the heritage that has been given to them. It is only the presence of God which will give our youth a desire to have the same dedication as their parents to the cause of Christ. I am thankful for the number of young people who have taken the way with God; yet, I must recognize that across the country, many churches are nearing the point of complete collapse.

Tragically the church is also seeing the loss of many people who were once the backbone of the local church. Some organizations have had numerous leaders leave their group then abandon their previous convictions.[12] The major causes behind these people leaving are either the loss of faith in the doctrine or the lifestyle, or contentions within the church. The fire of the Holy Spirit is the only answer to these problems. A lukewarm church which has not personally experienced God's presence cannot fervently believe or preach truth. Furthermore, when a church has God's presence, lifestyle issues become secondary to pleasing God. Without the Spirit the church easily devolves into quarreling between the members. Continual strife in a church is evidence of carnal people (1 Cor 3:3), but Christians should be known by their "love one to another" (John 13:35).

Very closely related to the loss of young families is the failure to successfully evangelize. Without the Spirit, a church will have few if any converts from the world that become fervent, old-fashioned people. Often those whom a church successfully reaches are only nominally committed to our beliefs and churches. Radical, Spirit-filled churches should always grow; this is our American religious heritage. The Methodists, Baptists, Holiness people, and Pentecostals all had their greatest growth when they were radically old-fashioned. It is this type of revival for which I pray—one which has the power of the Spirit to break across denominational lines and even doctrines, turning the hearts of all to fervently live the Bible in obedience to God. It is thrilling to see a new person converted, but it seems the church has lost much of its ability to evangelize and transform those from the world. I completely agree with the words written in a song by the Jerald Glick family, "It's the glory that will bring lost souls to kneel at Calvary."[13] If

---

12. Quite a number of leaders left the Church of God (Holiness) during the 1980s and 1990s, including some of the general leaders. These men left to join a more liberal group. This has also been true of some of the other denominations in the Conservative Holiness Movement.

13. Glick, "I'm Contending for the Glory," 61.

it is the glory that will bring souls in, it is also true that the lack of the glory will lead to the lack of success in evangelism.

In short, the church is dying. If the current trends continue, our message will begin to disappear in many communities. We live in a sin-cursed world, and every church door that closes is another place where hope of deliverance disappears. I wholeheartedly agree with the two general moderators of the Bible Missionary Church who stated in their 2003 report: "Go all out for revival at every level. It seems this is not an option. We must see revival—a deep, soul-searching, sin-killing, church blessing time when the saints humble themselves before the Almighty, pray, fast, and believe until He comes to rain righteousness upon us."[14] Since the time in which this call was made it has become even more desperate. Without revival there will be no survival.

---

14. Bible Missionary Church, *Fourteenth General Conference Journal*, 99–100.

CHAPTER 5

The Sociological Causes of Church Growth

The church is not an isolated organization that does not have ties to other sociological movements. The same sociological underpinnings that affect political parties, businesses, fads, and charitable organizations also affect the church. The same reasons why people are attracted to other ideologies or organizations can help explain why people are attracted to a church. The church as a sociological organization has attracted the attention of sociologists, especially after the decline of the mainline churches beginning in the sixties and the concurrent rise of evangelical churches. As sociologists have tried to analyze and understand the societal forces which cause some movements to grow and others to shrink, I have identified several key concepts which they gave as necessary for denominational growth.

THESE KEY PRINCIPLES ARE:

- The denomination must be strict. It must be different from and stricter than society-at-large in some ways. Sociologists often use the term "stigmata" to refer to these divergent behaviors.
- The denomination must be evangelistic. Rather than becoming insular and isolating itself from society, the group takes its message and defends it to outsiders with the hopes of evangelizing them to their doctrine and church.

- The denomination must be absolutist regarding its beliefs and practices. Other groups outside of its belief system are considered as lost.
- Another ingredient which has a major effect upon some groups is the fertility rate of the people in the group. The fertility rate is the major factor in the growth of some American groups such as the Amish. Worldwide this is a major factor in the numerical growth for Muslims.

There are many other factors which affect church and denominational growth, especially at the local level. The personal dynamics of individual pastors and their leadership ability are of key importance and lead to local success, but often cannot be replicated by differing personalities in other localities. While the Church Growth movement among evangelicals has focused mainly upon the growth of individual churches, sociology has focused predominantly upon denominations. It would seem the same principles which would lead a local church to succeed would work for entire denominations; however, this does not seem to be true. In fact, it sometimes seems to be in contradiction.

Sociological studies have repeatedly shown denominations and belief systems which are strict in their theology and demanding in behavior are the groups which grow. In contrast, megachurches are often built upon downplaying doctrine and rigid requirements. Megachurches focus upon finding out what the unchurched in that area desire and then fulfill that want. Growing denominations, in contrast, are at odds with the culture, emphasize their differences, and give little room for cultural accommodation.

Concepts from the Church Growth movement and the megachurch model of growth have dominated Church Growth methodology for the last several decades. Occurring simultaneously with the rise of the Church Growth movement among conservative churches has been the decline in growth in these same denominations. Statistically, it seems the Church Growth movement has undermined church growth. However, numerous successful churches have been established which have exploded in numbers; but in spite of many individual successes, church growth has collapsed, and the American church is dying. Many of the ideas promoted are excellent concepts which should be encouraged by all churches desiring growth. The problem is that the underlying principle of cultural accommodation and being seeker-sensitive has eroded the very foundation of Christianity. Charismatic personalities have been capable of building the large church, but it is evident that current growth theories among evangelicals failed to produce an answer for the average or small church to succeed. It was anticipated that the new interest in church growth would lead to an explosion in church attendance; instead, the opposite has occurred, and numerical decline among evangelicals has resulted. If scientific sociological studies are correct, the megachurch model is the cause of the problem instead of the solution; accordingly, the more effort most small churches place into emulating the methodology of megachurches, the faster the decline of those churches will occur. Without the doctrinal moorings holding attendees in the small church, these people will also depart for the excitement of the large church.

THE STRICTNESS THEORY

The assumption that high demands would limit the number who join an organization is reasonable; yet the opposite is true. People are looking for a worthy cause to dedicate their lives to rather than a cheap religion which demands little and is accordingly little valued.[1] In 1972, Dean Kelley proposed what was, at that time, a radical revision of common thought. Kelley, a Methodist pastor and an official in the National Council of Churches, studied the problem of growth from the perspective of the collapse of the mainline churches in the 1960s, contrasting them to the growth rates of evangelical and conservative churches. In spite of his dislike of the results of his study, Kelley presented his conclusions in a bold, dramatic fashion.

In Kelley's book, *Why Conservative Churches Are Growing*, he gave what he called a "recipe for failure of the religious enterprise."[2] These concepts stand in almost complete contradiction to what is commonly believed as the best way to achieve church growth.

KELLEY'S RECIPE FOR CHURCH FAILURE:

[The church will]

- Be reasonable, rational, courteous, responsible, restrained, and receptive to outside criticism; that is they will want to preserve a good image in the eyes of the world . . .
- Be gentle and democratic in their internal affairs. . .
- Be responsive to the needs of men (as currently conceived), and will want to work cooperatively with other groups to meet those needs. . .
- Not let dogmatism, judgmental moralism, or obsessions with cultic purity stand in the way of such cooperation and service.[3]

1. Finke and Stark, *Churching of America, 1776–1990*, 249–254.
2. Kelley, *Why Conservative Churches Are Growing*, viii.
3. Kelley, *Why Conservative Churches Are Growing*, vii–viii.

Kelley proposed that

> contrary to the prevailing sociological assumptions of secularization and modernization . . . parishioners are not, in fact, attracted to the inclusivism and tolerance provided by liberal groups and that, instead, they long for a robust sense of meaning that can only be found in high-expectation, high-commitment, and necessarily conservative religion.[4]

To prove his thesis, Kelley systematically compared growth rates between mainline churches and evangelical churches. He noted, "In the latter years of the 1960s, something remarkable happened in the United States: for the first time in the nation's history most of the major church groups stopped growing and began to shrink."[5] While these churches had lost market share as a percentage of church attendees in the United States, the actual attendance in "most of these denominations had been growing uninterruptedly since colonial times."[6] Kelley contended "that the mainline churches were declining not because they asked too much of their members but because they asked too little."[7]

> Churches decline not because they asked too much of their members but because they asked too little. —Dean Kelley

The strictness thesis, as this was called, was vehemently challenged by other scholars who did not like the analysis. Some argued the losses were only a result of the cultural crisis of the sixties. Others challenged the statistics, while some developed the idea that it was easier for a smaller group to grow rather than a larger one.[8]

In spite of initial objections, time has provided undeniable evidence of the correlation between strictness and growth, and "statistical studies have confirmed that denominational growth rates correlate strongly with 'strictness' and its concomitants."[9] Kelley's observations have proven to be startlingly correct. Mainline churches have continued the downward trek. Most of the great denominations upon which America was founded are closing churches and rapidly losing membership. These denominations

---

4. Thomas and Olson, "Testing the Strictness Thesis," 619.
5. Kelley, *Why Conservative Churches Are Growing*, 1.
6. Kelley, *Why Conservative Churches Are Growing*, 1.
7. Finke and Stark, *Churching of America, 1776–1990*, 249.
8. Finke and Stark, *Churching of America, 1776–1990*, 246–48.
9. Iannaccone, "Why Strict Churches Are Strong," 1181.

include the Episcopal Church (Anglican), United Church of Christ (formerly Congregationalists and Puritans), the Presbyterian Church, the United Methodist Church, and the more liberal Baptist and Lutheran churches. The major exception of America's larger denominations was the Southern Baptist Convention, which continued to maintain a more conservative tradition. The following chart shows the decline of the more liberal, larger Protestant denominations in the country.[10]

Membership numbers given in millions

Denomination	1968	1988	2008	percent of decline 1968—2008
Episcopal Church	3.4	2.5	2.1	38 percent
Evangelical Lutheran Church	5.8	5.3	4.6	21 percent
Presbyterian Church	4.1	3.0	2.8	32 percent
United Church of Christ	2.0	1.6	1.1	45 percent
United Methodist Church	11.0	9.0	7.7	30 percent

While Kelley's book brought the problem to the forefront of thinking, ominous signs among mainline churches had been occurring for decades. "Historical research has revealed that the mainline's share of the church-going population has been declining since the American Revolution."[11] As long as actual membership kept rising, these facts were ignored. The losses of the 1960s shocked the mainline churches into a reality check. Scholars scrambled to explain the "sudden decline of the liberal denominations and the sudden 'resurgence' of evangelical groups."[12] Many scholars focused upon the cultural changes and turmoil of the 1960s as the cause of the sudden downturn and missed the long-term trends; however, since the beginning of the country, the more conservative and aggressive denominations have been outpacing other denominations in the market share of those in the country who attended church.[13] The more liberal churches had been losing out competitively for a long time. As Roger Finke and Rodney Stark noted, "It would be pointless to search the 1960s for the causes of a phenomenon that was far along by the War of 1812."[14]

10. http://www.thearda.com/Denoms/D_1463.asp.
11. Iannaccone, "Why Strict Churches Are Strong," 1181. http://citeseerx.ist.psu.edu/viewdoc/download?doi=10.1.1.475.6086&rep=rep1&type=pdf.
12. Finke and Stark, *Churching of America, 1776–1990*, 246.
13. Finke and Stark, *Churching of America, 1776–1990*, 247.
14. Finke and Stark, *Churching of America, 1776–1990*, 249.

The study of the history of American churches in *The Churching of America* by Finke and Stark has identified that more aggressive conservative denominations have constantly overtaken mainstream denominations in America. The United States has had a constantly changing religious landscape, with churches moderating their positions and then being passed by more demanding groups. "To the degree that denominations . . . ceased to make serious demands on their followers, they ceased to prosper. The churching of America was accomplished by aggressive churches committed to vivid otherworldliness."[15] The Puritan, Anglican, and Presbyterian denominations which dominated the landscape of America in colonial days were overtaken by the Methodists, the Baptists, and the Catholics. In the twentieth century, the evangelicals and Pentecostals began to overtake all of the mainline denominations.

Evangelicals have followed the same pattern as other groups, have lost their strictness and their ability to grow; consequently they have begun to decline just as the mainline churches did in the 1960s. The major replacement for people today, however, is not stricter groups; instead, many are dropping out of attending church, or completely abandoning all religious beliefs.

No longer do evangelicals make demands upon their people. According to the current evangelical beliefs, strictness does not matter. Once a person is saved, he or she is always saved; it does not matter what they do. Whether a person attends church, pays tithe, or lives a wicked, immoral life, he or she is guaranteed entrance into heaven. Charles Stanley expressed it well when he said, "It is not lying, cheating, stealing, raping, murdering, or being unfaithful that sends people to hell."[16] This new Calvinistic theology does advocate a godly lifestyle, but its adherents consider that behavior is unrelated to eternal salvation. Neo-Calvinists state that "believers who lose or abandon their faith will retain their salvation, for God remains faithful."[17] This is a relatively new development in evangelical theology. Until recently it was emphasized that when a person was converted, he or she lived a changed life. The old-time Calvinists were some of the holiest people that have ever lived on this earth. They were known for their "pursuit of purity,"[18] and believed if a person did not become a new creature as was evidenced by their lifestyle, he or she had never been truly born again. This new twist

---

15. Finke and Stark, *Churching of America, 1776–1990*, 1.
16. Charles Stanley, quoted in Corner, *Believer's Conditional Security*, 182.
17. Charles Stanley, quoted in Corner, *Believer's Conditional Security*, 117.
18. The fundamentalists were so identified with their godly lives that one book about them was titled *In Pursuit of Purity*.

on eternal security doctrine has broken the connection between behavior—including church attendance—and salvation. Since neo-Calvinists believe church attendance is irrelevant to eternal salvation, church membership and attendance have begun to decline. After all, why get out of bed, or why not do something else, if attendance does not matter? Evangelical groups have gone the same route as the mainline denominations did in the sixties. They have lost their strictness and have also lost their growth. Kelley gave some minimal maxims of strictness that would be necessary for growth. Several of these are:

- Make high demands of those admitted to the organization that bears the faith, and do not include or allow to continue within it those who are not fully committed to it.
- Do not consent to, encourage, or indulge any violations of its standards of belief or behavior by its professed adherents.
- Do not keep silent about it, apologize for it, or let it be treated as though it made no difference, or should make no difference, in their behavior or in their relationship with others.[19]

Other scholars have also noted the correlation between strictness and religious growth. In a 2017 study of commitment relating to religious growth, Prosper Raynold noted "the extraordinary effectiveness of extremist religious sects such as Hamas, Hezbollah, and the Taliban."[20] While the strictness theory has been accepted as the best explanation for the growth of conservative churches in the late twentieth century, it has been more difficult to explain the reasons. Kelley believed that, contrary to what was commonly thought, religious enterprises will fail which are "reasonable, rational, courteous, responsible, restrained, and receptive to outside criticism; that is, they will want to preserve a good image in the world (as the world defines all these terms.)"[21] Kelley also noted that groups which do grow believe they "have the truth and all others are in error . . . are intolerant of deviance or dissent," and have a "shared stigmata [standards] of belonging."[22]

The value of strictness strengthens "a church in three ways: they raise overall levels of commitment, they increase average rates of participation, and they enhance the net benefits of membership."[23] These demands help

---

19. Kelley, *Why Conservative Churches Are Growing*, 121.
20. Raynold, "Economic Theory of Religious Affiliation," 5.
21. Kelley, *Why Conservative Churches Are Growing*, 84.
22. Kelley, *Why Conservative Churches Are Growing*, 84.
23. Iannacone, "Why Strict Churches Are Strong," 1183.

provide meaning to a member's life. It brings a new identity that ties a person into what is believed to be a valuable cause; accordingly, the high demands and stigmatas are willingly met. "The quest for meaning produces religious strictness, religious strictness produces congregational strength, and congregational strength produces congregational growth."[24]

Numerous studies have proven the validity of Kelley's basic premise. One of these, by Jeremy Thomas and Daniel Olson, published in 2010 from information taken from the U.S. Congregational Life Survey (2001), found "significant support for the mechanisms at the core . . . of the strictness thesis, particularly that even after controlling for the other dynamics mentioned, congregational strictness has both an indirect and a direct positive effect on congregational growth."[25] This study isolated out other variables to determine if strictness alone had a positive effect upon growth, and it showed there was a "direct positive effect of strictness on growth. . . . Strict rules may, in fact, have some degree of innate attraction, perhaps due in part to social-psychological reasons."[26] The evangelical beliefs and behavior of people in a church "necessarily go hand in hand in the production of congregational strength and ultimately of congregational growth."[27] The study of Thomas and Olson concluded that after forty years of debate "strict rules remain positively associated with congregational growth" along with evangelical theology and fertility.[28]

The church denominations which grow are those who challenge the accepted norms of the American culture, while those which identify with and fit in with the American culture decline. Individual churches sometimes will be outliers depending upon the leadership and ability of a local church, but this is not true of national organizations. Growing denominations attack the dominant culture and vigorously defend their reasons for their differences.

UNDERSTANDING WHY STRICT CHURCHES GROW

Once sociologists recognized the tie between denominational growth and strictness, studies were undertaken to determine why this was true. One of the most accepted theories is "Strictness makes organizations stronger and more attractive because it reduces free riding. It screens out members who

---

24. Thomas and Olson, "Testing the Strictness Thesis," 619.
25. Thomas and Olson, "Testing the Strictness Thesis," 619.
26. Thomas and Olson, "Testing the Strictness Thesis," 635.
27. Thomas and Olson, "Testing the Strictness Thesis," 636.
28. Thomas and Olson, "Testing the Strictness Thesis," 637.

lack commitment and stimulates participation among those who remain."[29] Laurence Iannaccone's perspective is that churches are driven by highly competitive market forces. People choose a religion based upon its ability to provide a "commodity at least as attractive as its competitors,"[30] yet the faster-growing religions have practices which, to an outsider, are completely irrational. This is true not only of American Protestantism but also Jewish groups and others such as the Mormons and Jehovah's Witnesses.[31] Why would someone choose to join a religion which seemed to make irrational demands? To the participant, the benefits of being part of a group must outweigh the costs. It must be in some way or another a rational decision.

Iannaccone's study assumed the personal satisfaction one had with his or her religion was based upon the personal enjoyment which he or she obtained as a result. Maximum returns occur when a person is committed and an enthusiastic participant. Since religion is a corporate experience that occurs within a collective group, the emotional level of the others also contributes to one's own personal edification. When a person is greeted warmly, takes part in a family atmosphere, joins in with others in excited singing and worship services, church is an enjoyable and satisfactory experience.[32] The reverse is also true. When religious services become routine and boring, the thrill of church is gone and the religious enterprise begins to decline.

The idea that churches grow by limiting the number of free-riders, however, does have some serious flaws. "Many religious groups, contrary to the spirit of screening and exclusion implied by the stigma-screening theory, are very welcoming to individuals who contribute little or nothing to the group."[33] Anyone who is familiar with evangelical churches knows great efforts are made to make outsiders feel welcome and accepted. In fact, reaching out to the unchurched is the major focus of many growing evangelical churches; their driving purpose is to reach the unsaved with the gospel message. These groups often "expend costly resources reaching out to these individuals,"[34] rather than spending the resources on things which would be of benefit to the members.[35]

A growing church must in some way or another attract those who are not of its constituency or the organization will stagnate and die. Sociologists

---

29. Iannaccone, "Why Strict Churches Are Strong," 1180.
30. Iannaccone, "Sacrifice and Stigma," 273.
31. Iannaccone, "Sacrifice and Stigma," 273.
32. Iannaccone, "Sacrifice and Stigma," 274.
33. McBride, "Why Churches Need Free-Riders," 2.
34. McBride, "Why Churches Need Free-Riders," 2–3.
35. McBride, "Why Churches Need Free-Riders," 2–3.

recognize that growth demands bringing in a number of free-riders to inculcate them into the organization, but many fail to understand the dynamics of how religious organizations grow at the grassroots level. Growing churches actually desire to pack the church building with potential converts which sociologists call free-riders. People who are members of growing churches believe the more unchurched there are in the building, the more potential there is for God to move on those people and change their lives. Growth demands a constant outreach to the spiritually needy. These people are invited into the church and "do, in fact, free-ride temporarily, but they are welcomed in the hope that they do not free-ride forever."[36]

Evangelicals do not question what benefit a free-rider would bring to the church. Their goal is to get unbelievers in contact with the truth so their lives may be transformed by the power of Christ. An evangelistic church has a burning desire to reach people with the gospel in order to save them from an eternal hell and to provide hope in this life. This is what drives evangelical churches. Other organizations outside Christian orthodoxy, which many would consider cults, follow similar sociological principles and are some of the fastest-growing religious organizations. Often the more stigmatas a group has, the more fervent and evangelistic the organization. It would seem that "the stricter, the stronger—within limits."[37] Strictness is just one factor involved in denominational growth. Sociological studies have identified the necessity for strictness, but there are other major factors which will be considered in the next chapters.

---

36. McBride, "Why Churches Need Free-Riders," 30.
37. Kelley, *Why Conservative Churches Are Growing*, 95.

CHAPTER 6

The Necessity of Evangelistic Theology

Evangelical theology is a key ingredient in growth since the effort in outreach is directly related to the number of new people which are attracted to a church.

One extensive study by David Roozen and C. Kirk Hadaway in *Church and Denominational Growth* admitted the correlation between strictness and growth, but contended there were other major factors which led to numerical growth. The explosive birthrate during the baby boom of the 1950s ended and "rates of membership growth dropped along with the birthrate and population growth."[1] This likely was the factor which led to the sudden drop of mainline churches in the 1960s; yet Roozen and Hadaway still admitted that "conservative denominations are still growing; the mainline is still in decline."[2] The authors attributed this partly to a higher birthrate among conservative churches and their location in growing areas of the country. But the authors admitted "these differences alone do not explain the numerical gap between conservative and mainline denominations."[3] Roozen and Hadaway did identify what they believed was one potential flaw in Kelley's theory; they noted it "fails to explain why strict, nonevangelical sects frequently experience very little growth."[4]

---

1. Roozen and Hadaway, *Church and Denominational Growth*, 39.
2. Roozen and Hadaway, *Church and Denominational Growth*, 41.
3. Roozen and Hadaway, *Church and Denominational Growth*, 41.
4. Roozen and Hadaway, *Church and Denominational Growth*, 42.

Their study attributed evangelistic action and a lower level of secularization as the reasons for numerical growth among conservative churches.[5]

Churches which grow have members with an evangelistic zeal and an "eagerness to tell the 'good news' of one's experience ... [and a] refusal to be silenced."[6] Groups that are strict but not evangelistic will see few outsiders come into their denominations or belief systems. If those groups who do not evangelize grow through a high fertility rate, there is little other impact upon the people in the culture. A key in promoting evangelism is viewing outsiders as lost. This type of absolutist theology is a necessity for a group to differentiate itself from other religious groups. One study of mainline churches in Canada showed that clergy in churches which were declining numerically "were more reserved about evangelism: none of them strongly agreed that it is very important to encourage non-Christians to become Christians, compared to 76.9 percent of growing church clergy."[7]

Scripture gives conservative Christians what they believe to be an authoritative basis for their purpose in evangelism and their strict lifestyle. These "Christian religions interpret the Bible as the Word of God and rely on biblical quotes to assert that its authors were inspired by the Holy Spirit or God."[8] Outsiders are seen as needing the truth which the participants in the church are willing to share. Clergy in growing churches "as a group exhibited the highest degree of theological conservatism,"[9] and believed their theology was an important key to their growth. Having a theology based upon the absolutes of the Bible is important to proclaiming the message of salvation with clarity and boldness. In one study half of the ministers who pastored growing churches stated, "the boldness of their message contributed to growth."[10] One minister noted that others "were afraid to say that Christ is unique and powerful and different than all other religions."[11]

COMPETITIVE MARKETING THEORY

The competitive marketing theory espoused by Roger Finke, Rodney Stark, and Laurence Iannaccone attempts to understand church growth from this sociological perspective. This theory focuses on studies of the development

---

5. Roozen and Hadaway, *Church and Denominational Growth*, 42.
6. Kelley, *Why Conservative Churches Are Growing*, 84.
7. Flatt et al., "Secularization and Attribution," 103.
8. Raynold, "Economic Theory of Religious Affiliation," 31.
9. Flatt et al., "Secularization and Attribution," 87.
10. Flatt et al., "Secularization and Attribution," 97.
11. Flatt et al., "Secularization and Attribution," 97.

of religion in American history. This macro-theory focuses upon religious entrepreneurs who:

> Capitalize on unregulated religious environments to aggressively market their religions to new consumers; in these environments, religious firms (denominations and traditions), that possess superior organizational structures (denominational polities), sales representatives (evangelists and clergy), products (religious messages), and marketing (evangelistic) techniques flourish. Those that do not cannot successfully compete and so decline numerically.[12]

Competitive marketing theory argues the effect of free market economics in religion has been good for religion as a whole but has also allowed upstart religions to overtake more established religious faiths. Older religious organizations lose their vitality and are overtaken by new denominations who aggressively market their faith. These groups usually make strict demands upon their members and grow rapidly. This has provided further evidence that Kelle's concept regarding strictness is correct; however, these two theories analyze church growth at different levels:

> Strictness theories locate the crucial variable determining religious vitality and weakness at the level of individual religious congregations and the demands they place on their members; competitive marketing theory, by contrast, focuses on macro religious economies and the incentives and opportunities they offer religious entrepreneurs to market their products.[13]

Christian Smith contends that "religion survives and can thrive in pluralistic, modern society by embedding itself in subcultures that offer satisfying morally orienting collective identities which provide adherents meaning and belonging."[14] In order for a group to thrive it must "possess and employ the cultural tools needed to create both clear distinction from and significant engagement and tension with other relevant outgroups."[15] Those groups which succeed are able to provide a sense of purpose to life and a social network with which a person identifies. The denomination must distinguish itself from other competing groups, yet at the same time it must clash with and engage outsiders in order to gain converts.

12. Smith, quoted in Finke and Stark, "Demographics of Religious Participation," 73.
13. Smith, *American Evangelicalism*, 74.
14. Smith, *American Evangelicalism*, 118.
15. Smith, *American Evangelicalism*, 119.

Evangelical churches have found a good mix within the competitive religious landscape of America. With dozens of denominations and thousands of independent churches, the United States has the availability of opportunity for leaders to try differing approaches until they find a successful method. Mainline denominations, to a great degree, operate within denominational boundaries that offer comparatively little opportunity for new ideas and young entrepreneurs with contrasting visions. The broad competitive field among the multitude of evangelical churches has allowed for new initiatives from charismatic visionaries. Evangelicalism has somehow managed to develop across a broad array of theological groupings to

> fairly successfully orient this medley of traditions and positions in a common direction with common purpose.... This relatively successful unity-in-diversity allows the evangelical tradition to capture the allegiance of and orient for active mission an incredibly broad array of Christians, while maintaining a tremendous degree of decentralization.[16]

The competitive marketing theory helps provide evidence that evangelism is important for denominational success. The more effective the evangelism techniques and the more incentive a denomination has to evangelize will be major factors in whether a denomination is successful or not. Some might even suggest this is perhaps the only major factor involved in determining church growth. Yet, at odds with this idea is the reality that many evangelical churches today, while still involved in outreach ministries, are struggling to successfully evangelize. The effective evangelistic methodology which was so effective a few years ago seems to be failing to propel the American church forward. As the lifestyle of the "Christians" in twenty-first-century churches deteriorates into open sin, it seems the foundations of the church are crumbling and even the power to attract numbers is disappearing or shrinking in most conservative churches.

Another set of theories has focused upon the economics involved in religious growth. Prosper Raynold conceives that "laypeople consider both religious rewards and risks in making affiliation decisions."[17] Churches grow based upon the level of confidence the people have regarding the capability of a religious belief to provide eternal benefits for themselves. This "production of supernatural hope—which is the fundamental motive for religiosity—requires costly compliance with [the] supernatural will."[18] The costs of compliance may include such things as "dietary restrictions, dress

---

16. Smith, *American Evangelicalism*, 87.
17. Raynold, "Economic Theory of Religious Affiliation," 2.
18. Raynold, "Economic Theory of Religious Affiliation," 32.

codes, limitations on social interaction, and other costly prohibitions."[19] The simple investing of a person's resources into a religious enterprise in which he feels is true and authoritative causes a person to become even more convinced of the validity of the belief system. A less costly religion with little investment lends toward a weak belief, while a costly religion demands fervent commitment. The enthusiasm of the constituents then encourages others to join that religion.

IMPORTANCE OF ABSOLUTIST THEOLOGY

A high level of absolutism regarding their beliefs is another characteristic of growing churches. Denominations which grow rapidly believe they have the truth and that "all others are in error."[20] It is this firm conviction of having the truth necessary for heaven which gives the "supernatural hope that is the dominant motive for religiosity."[21] A growing church believes their beliefs and practices are necessary for heaven and sees outsiders as people who are lost and in need of the gospel. The overriding drive of the members is to share the good news, and often a person will give much of their time and finances to achieve that objective. When a person is converted, their effort is validated and leads to even increased fervent activity to transform other lives. A member's life then takes on new meaning and purpose. He believes God is using him to help others and transform his world.

This has also been true of past movements. Revivalistic groups such as the Methodist Church could not have paid their circuit riders to have made the sacrifices they did, but their leader, Francis Asbury, had inspired them with his vision to reach the country for Christ. Asbury himself traveled "nearly 300,000 miles on horseback, disregarding weather and chronic ill-health, to supervise his far-flung network of itinerants and circuit riders."[22] The Methodists of that day saw people as lost souls in need of the gospel and were convinced their specific message was what the people needed.

Groups which have shown rapid growth historically are those who were willing to publicly defend their message. Growth in the early church occurred as the apostles filled Jerusalem with their doctrine (Acts 5:28) and publicly convinced Jews that Jesus was the Christ (Acts 18:28). Rapid growth characterized such groups as the Lutherans, the Calvinists, and the Anabaptists at the time of the Reformation. Each of these followed the same

---

19. Raynold, "Economic Theory of Religious Affiliation," 32–33.
20. Kelley, *Why Conservative Churches Are Growing*, 79.
21. Raynold, "Economic Theory of Religious Affiliation," 8.
22. Finke and Stark, *Churching of America, 1776–1990*, 83.

basic approach: all of them fervently believed in their theological message and worked to convince others of its validity. The Wesleyan revival followed the same path. The Holiness movement has the same heritage. A little more than a century ago, Holiness theology was spreading throughout America. Its success was characterized by an emphasis on the distinctive doctrine of holiness. Evangelicals grew by emphasizing the necessity of the new birth. Pentecostal groups effectively reached out by emphasizing the speaking in tongues and miracles. Quasi-Christian groups or cults which are currently experiencing growth are also quick to emphasize their differences. Long-term growth demands an identification which distinguishes a group from other religious groups in society and a willingness to defend and promote those distinguishing traits.

> Groups which grow are those who are willing to publicly defend their message.

CHAPTER 7

Why Strict Groups May Fail

Strict denominations who fail to grow often no longer fervently believe the message of their founders. According to Arnold Cook, "The vision of the founders has faded, yet the organizational machinery grinds on."[1] Richard Niebuhr noted "the second generation holds its convictions less fervently than pioneers of the sects . . . with each succeeding generation, isolation from the world becomes more difficult."[2] This problem has occurred among some of the fundamentalist Baptists, radical Pentecostals, or conservative Holiness people. The Conservative Holiness movement (called CHM) maintains a very strict lifestyle but has followed the pattern of "historical drift" as diagnosed by Cook. Their churches have lost much of the fervency for their beliefs, and the movement is struggling to define the purpose for their existence as compared to the larger evangelical or Holiness movements.

THE CONSERVATIVE HOLINESS MOVEMENT

Being strict and maintaining the standards (or stigmatas as would be used by sociologists) which came from their heritage should be causing rapid growth in the CHM, but it has not. According to a study by Michael Avery, hardly any of the best CHM churches are seeing evangelistic growth.[3] Although

---

1. Cook, *Historical Drift*, 11.
2. Niebuhr, quoted in Cook, *Historical Drift*, 12.
3. Avery and Smith, *Call*, 165. In a blind study of thirty-three of the leading churches

there have been efforts made to address the problem, the Conservative Holiness movement's rate of numerical decline continues.[4] The underlying cause of the decline is that many in the movement no longer believe in the necessity of the original purpose of the group. Even a number of churches and denominations in the CHM are in transition to less strict behavioral guidelines; thus, they are abandoning the very reason why the movement began in the 1950s and 1960s.[5] A number of influential leaders have abandoned the conservatives. The acceptance of those outside the movement as genuine Christians who violate all of the key standards has undermined the belief in the necessity of their practices and doctrine. Even some of the church leaders feel that CHM beliefs and practices are no more than cultural customs carried over from the 1950s and 1960s. According to Dean Kelley, strong churches which grow have a "belief that 'we have the truth and all others are in error,'" and they are intolerant "of deviance or dissent."[6]

The very basic concept of being judgmental is anathema to most CHM people and makes them very uncomfortable. Most of those in the CHM do not outspokenly condemn the behavior and doctrine of those outside the movement; however, whether it is comfortable or not, it is still the cause of the slow death of the group. One excellent example of this concept was a question-and-answer session at a general gathering of young people. The question was asked, "If other Christians are going to heaven without the standards that we believe, why can't we believe like them?"[7] The answer

from fifteen different denominations and four independent churches, only three of the churches had successfully evangelized in the last five years. 80 percent "have had no unchurched person converted and discipled to the level of membership within the last five years."

4. I have compared the attendance at the same churches over a ten-year period in seven different CHM denominations. All of the denominations except one had more churches with a declining Sunday school attendance than had a growing attendance. There was also a decline in the total number of attendees in Sunday school. Morning worship attendance did seem to be doing better, but most groups did not have these statistics. Two other groups had a way to measure attendance, and both of these were also showing decline. All of these groups also declined in the total number of churches in the denomination. The one exception was the Bible Holiness Church led by Stephen Kirkman, which gained both in churches and average attendance. The Evangelical Wesleyan Church also gained in number of churches, but I do not know if it had gained in average church attendance.

5. A number of the denominations are now doing things that their group once banned. Often the rules have not changed, they are just ignored, or laypeople do not become members.

6. Kelley, *Why Conservative Churches Are Growing*, 79.

7. West Harrison, Indiana. Youth Challenge, Afternoon session, October 26, 2018. The speaker's reply to the question is a good example of their beliefs and would have been similar to most others in the movement.

given by the speaker would have been typical of many other leaders in the group. He accepted the premise that these "biblical guidelines" were not necessary for others and never maintained that these standards were even necessary for CHM people. He also stated that he still identified those as Christians who had changed from a conservative lifestyle to more liberal practices, stating they had probably never understood the truth. His position was "we ought to stop unchristianizing people unless they violate" basic Christian orthodox doctrine or blatantly sin with unrepentant attitudes.[8]

The CHM began over their insistence regarding the importance of a number of key issues in which the culture and the church were changing. The CHM believed then that keeping this holy lifestyle was what God desired for everyone who was a Christian. They believed God would lead all who truly knew and loved God into these distinctives. Now if the leaders, however, no longer fervently believe in the basic purpose and heritage of the group, it is no wonder the youth are abandoning these conservative denominations and going to less strict churches. As Dean Kelley has noted, "Membership gain or loss is used as a useful . . . indicator of social strength."[9] It is evident the CHM has lost much of the social strength and growth it once had. In some instances the movement has reached beyond its ranks in its association with others outside its belief system. Some of this is needed and is not a theological or organizational threat, but in other ways the association with outsiders may be causing the CHM to lose its core values. In identifying the keys which lead to strength for an organization, Kelley said:

- A group is not inclined to cooperate with other groups until it has lost many of the traits of strictness that accompany and conserve social strength.

- A group that begins to cooperate with other groups will begin to lose any traits of strictness or evidences of social strength it may still have.

- For all practical purposes, there is no means by which the deterioration of social strength in a given organization can be slowed or arrested except by a reassertion of strictness.[10]

Another potential problem for the CHM is the failure to emphasize their differences in evangelism. Often people in the world have lost faith in the church and are looking for something more radical or different. Yet, the people in the movement downplay their standards in evangelism. Often

---

8. Youth Challenge, Afternoon session, 10-26-2018.
9. Kelley, *Why Conservative Churches Are Growing*, 95.
10. Kelley, *Why Conservative Churches Are Growing*, 132.

God does lead new converts to adopt the CHM practices, but the outcome of this philosophy has been to deemphasize how often and how emphatically standards are preached to all the people. Without the basis for their existence being constantly reiterated, the belief in the necessity of their distinctives has not become internalized in new converts or in the younger generation. Not only does this lack of emphasis hinder outreach, it also has led to a new generation being raised without the foundations of their belief system being properly laid. Accordingly, many CHM people are abandoning their strict background and leaving the church. The struggles of the CHM give an example of strict groups who fail to successfully grow. Similar examples could be given for other strict groups in other theological grids.

Growing radical groups constantly evangelize based upon their differences from other religious groups. They are "filled with missionary zeal to tell others the Good News of the meanings they have found and refuse to be silenced even at the price of suffering or death."[11] Seventh-day Adventists emphasize the day of worship; Pentecostals emphasize speaking in tongues; United Pentecostals are emphatic about their opposition to the doctrine of the Trinity; Jehovah's Witnesses immediately challenge others based upon their difference in the interpretation of Scripture. These groups are all growing based upon the emphasis of their distinctive doctrine.

When the Holiness movement was growing, it emphatically preached the doctrine of holiness, often stating it was either holiness or hell. The emphasis upon the doctrine of holiness has declined, and the doctrine in some places has been changed to a less radical relational concept; accordingly, the growth of the Holiness movement in the United States has stopped.

Evangelicals grew based upon their belief in the necessity of a new birth experience and the inerrancy of the Bible. Their religion has softened as the concept of repentance has been deemphasized or even stripped from the doctrine of the new birth. The eternal security belief, as often taught, opposes the necessity of any demands upon Christians by calling it legalism. Even the dogmatic stand regarding biblical inerrancy has weakened, especially the creation story. The American church has seen its foundations crumble. It has exchanged a solid foundation on the rock for shifting sand. All that is left is for the storm to strike, and the house that was once solid will fall.

WHAT IS THE ANSWER?

Church growth has always been based on whether the constituents of a religious organization believe the group has a reason to exist and how strongly

11. Kelley, *Why Conservative Churches Are Growing*, 81.

and exclusively their doctrines are held by the people in the church. One study from the 1930s showed "growing churches perceive substantial religious differences between themselves and others (which justifies their efforts to bring in new members)."[12] It is a historical aberration for the radical conservative movements in each of the belief systems to be struggling with decline. Normally strict groups grow. Only when the radical conservatives find a way to evangelize based upon their differences from the church world at large will they once again have success in evangelism. Trying to use a watered-down evangelical message to sell a radical lifestyle is not working and will never work. If what a group believes is valid, they should be able to convince others based on the merits of their beliefs. This is only true, however, if the group doing the convincing truly believes in their own message.

In the larger Holiness movement, the Church of the Nazarene was growing until after the beginning of the twenty-first century, but has suddenly hit a wall. The theological change which is occurring over their doctrine of holiness is a major part of the problem. As relational holiness theology spread from its inception in the early 1970s, its rise closely correlated with the decline of growth in the Holiness movement. This decline fits perfectly with sociological studies which emphasize that as a denomination loses its strictness it loses its social strength and growth. According to Mark Quanstrom, "At the end of the 20th century, there was no substantial agreement in the denomination over what it meant to be 'entirely sanctified.' The Church of the Nazarene no longer had a precisely articulated definition of their distinctive doctrine, the doctrine that at one time had been their sole reason for being."[13] Holiness was the message. Without it the Church of the Nazarene has lost its purpose for existence. When the denomination preached holiness and lived a life above willful sin, the movement grew. If the Nazarenes and other holiness churches have a future in the United States it will only be because they reemphasize their Wesleyan-Arminian beliefs of a life without willful sin and their belief about the transforming power of God to deal with the sin nature. These doctrines distinguish holiness people from other church denominations. If holiness people in America fail to articulate and live according to their heritage, they will become just another has-been religious group that has become part of the hedonistic, materialistic, quasi-Christian religious mush that today is called Christianity.

---

12. Finke and Stark, *Churching of America, 1776–1990*, 233.
13. Quanstrom, *Century of Holiness Theology*, 174.

THE VALUE OF COSTLY RELIGION

The most successful denominations in America today are those organizations which have what would be considered a strict lifestyle. Some of these are cults or are outside the mainstream of orthodox Christianity, but they have mastered the sociological concepts of evangelizing outsiders to their belief system. Two of the fastest-growing denominations in the United States today are the Seventh-day Adventists and the Jehovah's Witnesses.[14] Among those who would be identified as evangelicals, Pentecostal churches are doing better than others. One article in *Christianity Today* tried to analyze why Pentecostals were growing from a sociological viewpoint. The article stated,

> It's harder to be a nominal Pentecostal—the beliefs of the movement tend to weed out nominalism. Because of what is happening in church and the community of faith, people tend not to just hang around as casual observers. Either you join in it, or you move on. Many join. Movements populated by nominals are usually in decline. Nominals don't populate Pentecostalism, so it grows.[15]

Sometimes holiness people feel like our distinctives hinder growth, but the article continued to state, "Their distinctives apparently aren't hindering their growth—their distinctives are propelling growth globally . . . People want a faith with flavor. . . . Some groups are trying to downplay their distinctives to be more acceptable. Who wants to duplicate that? Nobody."[16]

> Some groups are trying to downplay their distinctives to be more acceptable. Who wants to duplicate that? Nobody. —Ed Stetzer

Christianity has always grown, not in spite of the high cost of membership, but because of it. This is the reason why persecution of the church does not kill it. People come to value that which costs. This should cause a person to question modern growth methodology, which has removed the cross from the gospel. Is it any wonder the power of the gospel to transform lives has also been lost? The common concept of growth now depends upon being culturally popular and providing programs, fellowship, and entertainment which may have little to do with Christianity. A church without a cost has ended up producing a populace that has little commitment. In some

---

14. Carpenter, "Adventist Church Reports."
15. Stetzer, "Why Do These Pentecostals Keep Growing?," paras. 9–10.
16. Stetzer, "Why Do These Pentecostals Keep Growing?," para. 22.

instances, this popularized Christianity has provided crowds who come for the show but exhibit little evidence that there is any long-term spiritual growth, even in the most successful churches. Loyalties to a denomination or the denomination's theological beliefs have never been developed or have been undermined. A megachurch could collapse into nothing just as quickly and easily as it grew. All it would take would be some problems in the local body of the church, and the people, without any theological moorings, could easily withhold their offerings or depart for another megachurch of a Baptist, Pentecostal, or mainline background. Accordingly, many large, entertainment-driven churches will eventually collapse.[17]

The issue of denominational growth has been thoroughly explored by dozens of studies in the last fifty years. Dean Kelley's book, *Why Conservative Churches Are Growing*, dropped the equivalent of a bomb into the liberal religious world. Religious scholars were outraged by the thought that their own denominations were shrinking while those groups that were despised were showing success. Almost fifty years have passed since Kelley's book challenged traditional sociological thinking concerning church growth. The evangelical churches, including Baptists, Holiness people, and Pentecostals, are now at the same crossroads. The formerly radical demands of a holy life have been stripped out of each group, and doctrine has been deemphasized to a generic religious hodgepodge that has little commitment to God. The exact same reasons why mainline churches in Europe and America began their trek toward irrelevance are the same reasons why evangelicals are struggling today. It seems the church has not learned from recent history and is tragically now on a course to repeat it. William J. Abraham said,

> As a serious experiment in theology, Wesleyanism is over. The wake may have been a long one, but the funeral is now upon us. To be sure, some are in denial and others are wrangling over the reading of the will and the ownership of the last legacy, but the reality is that Wesleyans have moved on and found new lives and lovers. . . . The Wesleyan tradition, like the earlier traditions spawned by the great Reformers before him, has gone the way of all flesh. Yet one more noble Protestant experiment has run its course. . . . Once more the faith of the church has been splintered in pieces and scattered to the winds. Once more it has been a case of death by our own hands.[18]

Abraham then goes ahead to say, "The death of our own tradition is simply a microcosm of the death of Protestantism itself. We are at the end

---

17. Dickerson, *Great Evangelical Recession*, 83.
18. Abraham, "End of Wesleyan Theology," 18–19.

of the line where Protestant theology is concerned; five hundred magnificent years of theology have come to an end."[19] Unless there are radical steps taken to reverse the slide the American Holiness movement is on, there is no future, and Abraham will be proven right.

---

19. Abraham, "End of Wesleyan Theology," 21.

CHAPTER 8

Biblical Foundations for Growth

Every answer the church needs for success lies in God's word. God certainly understood our day and the difficulties the church would face. Accordingly, Scripture should be studied to discover how to meet the challenges of our day. "Back to the Bible" should be no trite phrase but a deep, underlying conviction that God has already shown the church the answers for our day. In reality, people throughout history have been much the same. The postmodernism of our day is similar to the skepticism of the Greco-Roman world; yet the early church probably had the greatest revival in history. The gospel exploded from 120 fervent believers on the day of Pentecost to tens of thousands within a few decades and then conquered the empire within 300 years. If a miracle of this magnitude happened once in a world similar to ours, it can happen again. The principles of evangelism established by the apostles in the book of Acts need to be rediscovered and applied to the church of today. In an antagonistic world which no longer believed in truth, the apostles used these key foundational stones to overcome paganism and convert their world.

A BURNING PASSION IN THEIR HEARTS

The key underlying ingredient in church growth is the level of fervency which people have about their church and their religious belief. Simply put: groups that contain excited people who believe in their doctrine grow, but those who do not believe in their message gradually die. In the book of Acts the people were so possessed by their beliefs that it was impossible for them to stay quiet. When Peter and John were confronted by the Sanhedrin for preaching the resurrection of Christ from the dead, they responded, "We cannot but speak the things which we have seen and heard" (Acts 4:20). Churches without fervency in their services have little ability to attract others, and their own young people will go to places with greater excitement. Many places have substituted entertainment and exciting programs, music, or speakers to replace the spiritual fervency which the organization once held. This may lead to short-term gains for those churches or denominations which successfully provide the excitement; but if the foundation is wrong, it will never work long term. Groups which were successful in transforming the lives of people and culture have always been successful in building deep-seated convictions within their constituents. The fervency of their beliefs and excitement about God have been the major attractions in keeping their own and evangelizing those around them.

A LOVE FOR GOD AND OTHERS

Love motivates people. We do what we love. It is not a chore or a burden; love takes sacrifice and work but makes it a joy, not a burden. Only a church possessed with the love of God can sustain the drive of evangelism. The power of the Holy Spirit changes those people who are filled with the Spirit of God. No longer are they self-focused, but are possessed of the love which God has for the spiritual needs of other people. Paul described his motivation thusly, "the love of Christ constraineth us" (2 Cor 5:14). The Spirit in our hearts brings a passion for the souls of other people, compelling us to do something. It was this same love which led Jesus to come to earth and die on the cross that men might be saved. A burning love for Christ and for others will possess those who have been transformed by the power of God. There will be a desire in the heart of every Christian to make an eternal difference. Without this love laypeople will have little concern for lost souls. This is the reason why many churches have had to turn to paid ministers to accomplish what laypeople once did. A few paid professionals can never achieve what a church filled with excited laypeople can. A portion of a poem by Bill McChesney who died as a martyr in the Congo in 1963 expresses that love and dedication.

> MY CHOICE
> I want my breakfast served at eight,
> with ham and eggs upon the plate;
> A well-broiled steak I'll eat at one;
> and dine again when day is done.

But then the Master I can hear,
in no uncertain voice, so clear,
I bid you come and follow Me,
the lonely Man of Galilee.

Birds of the air have made their nest,
and foxes in their holes find rest;
But I can offer you no bed;
no place have I to lay My head.

In shame I hung my head and cried.
How could I spurn the Crucified?
Could I forget the way He went,
the sleepless nights in prayer He spent?

If he be God and died for me,
No sacrifice too great can be
For me, a mortal man, to make;
I'll do it all for Jesus' sake.

Yes, I will tread the path he trod,
No other way will please my God;
So, henceforth, this my choice shall be,
My choice for all eternity.[1]

A POWERFUL PERSONAL SENSE OF RESPONSIBILITY

Paul cried out from the depths of his heart, "Woe is unto me, if I preach not the gospel!" (1 Cor 9:16). He was consumed with reaching the lost. It was impossible for him to not speak up. He saw people as lost souls headed for eternity. The passion to save people drove every aspect of his life. How do we see people? Are we content to drift through life making no difference for eternity? The church of our day is filled with contented, undisturbed, happy people living for the materialism of this world. Yet, all around us the lost are marching into eternity without God. We should be shaken by the desperate need, but often we do not care.

It is also a command of God to do our part to evangelize. Obedience and duty demand a response. This is true whether there is any success or not; we are still commanded to go. Jesus told his disciples, "Go ye into all

---

1. McChesney, *Through Congo Shadows*, 10.

the world, and preach the gospel to every creature," and "Go ye therefore, and teach all nations" (Mark 16:15; Matt 28:19). In Matthew 25, the man who was only given only one talent was still expected to do something with what he had been given. When he failed to do anything he was called a "wicked and slothful servant . . . and cast . . . into outer darkness" (vv. 26, 30). Anyone who does not follow the commands of Christ on this issue will certainly face the judgment of God over their failure.

Failure to warn the wicked will also mean a person is personally responsible for not giving them warning. God stated if a person did not speak "to warn the wicked . . . his blood will I require at thine hand" (Ezek 3:18). Simple decency demands that if a person sees another headed to a disaster, he must be warned. Ezekiel uses the concept that God's people are watchmen whose job is to warn the people upon the approach of an enemy. Staying quiet and allowing the city to be taken without any defense would place the blood of those who died on the hands of the city guard who did not speak to warn the people. How can the people of God, if we truly believe in an eternal hell, remain quiet and allow our family, friends, and neighbors to perish without warning? If a person remains quiet about eternity, God will require their blood at our hands.

A GODLY PRIDE OF THE GOSPEL

A good, godly sense of pride in what Christ has done should dominate a Christian's thinking. God has transformed his life and given him a home in heaven. No Christian should fear the embarrassment to publicly identify as a Christian, but should be excited and cheerful to identify with Christ. We have the answer to the needs of our world, and we are part of the greatest thing this world has ever seen. As Paul stated, "I am not ashamed of the gospel of Christ: for it is the power of God unto salvation to every one that believeth" (Rom 1:16). What has happened to modern Christianity? No genuine Christian should want to look or act in any way that does not clearly identify them with Christ and his church. Yet, many who would claim to be saved act as if it is a stigma to be publically identified as a Christian. No wonder the sinner has little interest in becoming a Christian when those who claim the name of Christ are ashamed of him.

How does the world view identification with their pet idols? No person who is a football fan is ashamed to be identified with his team. His vehicle will have identifying bumper stickers, team flags will be flying from his house, and he will know all the statistics related to his team. If he would visit the opposing team's stadium, he would wear colors, shirts, and caps proudly identifying his team. The fans for the opposing team would hate and despise that identification, but he is a football fanatic. ("Fan" is short for "fanatic.") He proudly cheers his team on to victory no matter what others think. All of this is done for a sport of little value other than some ambiguous psychological feeling.

The change in Western culture in the last few decades means Christians are now readily identified by their looks and actions. Anytime a person does not fit in with the people around them, there is a level of peer pressure to conform to society. Yet, why should the people in the church change to get the approval of those who do not know God? Instead, identification should be used as a means of evangelization. Never forget, God's people are headed for an eternity in heaven while those of the world are headed for the judgment.

A proper pride of the transforming power of the gospel will enable a person to persevere in spite of difficulties. If something is considered valuable, a person keeps it and does not lose it. If it is lost, all efforts are made to recover the valuable item. Being convinced of the value and validity of his belief system, a person will pay whatever price he must to obtain and keep his religion. If he fails God because of temptation, he then fights his way back to victory. If the local church has problems, he does not quit. What he has is bigger than the church's problems. He sticks with his church rather than running to the popular church down the street that teaches another doctrine. In the worst-case scenario, he may switch to another local church of the same belief or start one of his own, but he is committed; he will not change. Furthermore, he will support his beliefs with his time and finances. He will also do whatever is necessary to make sure his family is indoctrinated in the same truth. But the opposite also occurs: if he is ashamed to be identified with his beliefs, he will use any excuse to quit. He will also not support that of which he is ashamed, nor will he care if his family becomes a part of it or not. When a person leaves the church and its doctrinal system, the true reason is seldom given and sometimes not even recognized. The church is normally blamed with any number of excuses such as: church fighting, rules with which they disagreed, personality clashes, etc. Yet, the underlying real reason lies in the failure to internalize the values and doctrines of the church of which they were a part.

A good pride in the gospel will give the church the power to propagate the message it believes in. No one is attracted to a group of people who are not sure who they are and who are not excited about what God has done for them. A firm certainty of the beliefs and power of the gospel, along with a boldness to emphasize the truth, is attractive. Unfortunately, it is not always people who have the truth who express certainty in their message. Sociologists have noticed that groups which grow are those who believe they have the answers, while those who are open-minded and unclear in their doctrine collapse. Those who have the truth should be excited about what the power of God has done for them and what it can do for other people. Any businessman knows in order to sell a product he must believe in that product himself. No matter how hard a person works trying to build his church, if he does not believe in his own message, any success will be only marginal and short term. If we have the truth, we must be convinced of it, be excited about it, and stand for what we believe in the marketplace of ideas.

A good pride will also help to purify the church of false doctrines and practices. A great shift in beliefs and practices has occurred in most doctrinal groupings, whether conservative or liberal. Liberal denominations have accepted gay marriage as legitimate and no longer believe in an inerrant Bible. Many evangelicals have accepted theistic evolution, and some are questioning the traditional beliefs regarding the doctrine of hell. As ministers have failed to preach and defend beliefs unpopular in society, their own constituencies have begun to doubt formerly strongly held positions. Instead of being proud of their beliefs, church people have become ashamed of their positions and have begun softening the most offensive doctrines and practices. Before long, children raised without a clear message, as well as some adults, will no longer believe the historical truths of the Scripture. Their denominations will have then begun the transformation to more culturally accepted positions, but they will also have lost their original purpose for existence.

Often it is believed that by removing the most offensive part of the gospel it will aid in reaching new people as well as keeping others from leaving the church. Instead, when a belief or practice is not defended strongly for a period of years, the people in the church begin questioning the importance of that doctrine. Not only does a lack of emphasis in beliefs cause a failure to grow, it also lays the seeds which undermine the doctrine or practices of the organization. Most of the change occurs without any noticeable difference. For a period of time, neither the beliefs nor the behavior of the people show any overt changes. What does occur, however, is an internal transformation. The people of that group no longer believe what the denomination once believed. Even those who still hold to the original doctrines do not believe them with the same fervency. Suddenly, within a few years the organization goes through a transformation. A few rebels lead the way, but then quickly the entire group follows. The organization then begins acclimating to the culture at large. At first only the most radical positions change, but within a few years a moderating course is established which is almost impossible to stop. Mainline denominations have already traveled this way; but over the last fifty years, evangelicals have now started down this road to nowhere. It is time to stop, reassess our direction, and make corrections to the course or we, too, will watch our church die.

CHAPTER 9

Identifying the Mission Field

THE GREAT COMMISSION

Jesus taught that the message of the gospel was for the whole world, but specifically where is an individual person's mission field? It is the job of Christians to win the whole world, but it is also our job to win our neighbor. Sometimes it is thought that evangelism is the job of the professional, such as the pastor; but Scripture is clear that it is the job of every Christian. In fact, each individual has those people whom he has a better opportunity to reach than any other person. A person's circle of family, friends, and co-workers are more likely to listen to the testimony of one whom they know rather than the message of a professional who is only doing the job for which he is paid.

The book of Acts teaches the necessity of evangelizing in one's own city (1:8). Each person must reach those people who live where they live. Initially the church evangelized in Jerusalem; but as persecution scattered the church following the death of Stephen, it says, "they that were scattered abroad went every where preaching the word" (Acts 8:4). The most powerful witness to the gospel is a zealous layman burning with a message that he shares wherever he goes. It is also the best way to establish new church plants. When laymen move to new areas, it gives a denomination a new core around which to build a church. This drive initially led Methodists to form new churches overseas. "In the British Colonies, Methodism began spontaneously. Converted immigrants and soldiers carrying on their lips the testimony of Jesus 'went everywhere preaching the word.' The seed thus carried soon took root on American, African, and Australian soil."[1]

Not only must our local vicinity be evangelized, but it is our responsibility to evangelize neighboring areas and around the world. John Wesley's vision infused the Methodists with a burning ambition to save souls. He said, "I look upon all the world as my parish; thus far I mean, that, in whatever part of it I am, I judge it meet, right, and my bounden duty to declare unto all that are willing to hear, the glad tidings of salvation. This is the work which I know God has called me to."[2] Francis Asbury transferred that same vision to America. When he arrived, Asbury was disappointed to see that "church discipline was lax, [and] some members had a casual attitude."[3] However, "Asbury was obsessed with the vision of an evangelized America. To remain in one spot, he thought, betrayed the genius of Methodism."[4] When Asbury died forty-five years later, the Methodist Church was the largest denomination in the country. It is this same zeal and obsession the church world needs today. We are living in a pagan America, but it seems the church cares but little.

The gospel should be taken to those who are the most receptive to the message. Jesus stated, "And whosoever shall not receive you, nor hear your words, when ye depart out of that house or city, shake off the dust of your feet" (Matt 10:14). Some ethnic groups or locations are open and receptive to the gospel and others are not. Our major focus should be to evangelize those places which will produce the greatest number of converts. Certainly, places and people which are the most resistant should not be forgotten, but the bulk of time and resources should be sent to those places where the gospel is having the most success.

Those in need are often some of the most receptive to the message of hope. This occurred most often in the Bible when a person was healed, but in the process of healing Christ often dealt with the problem of sin. We live in a broken world; hurting people are all around us. Christ can meet the needs of broken people. He is able to give not only physical healing, but also able to heal the brokenhearted. If a person can trust God with their problems, he has promised that "the peace of God, which passeth all understanding, shall keep your hearts and minds through Christ Jesus" (Phil 4:7). Paul testified that "I have learned, in whatsoever state I am, therewith to be content" (Phil 4:11). The same power that could give Paul comfort in prison

---

1. Andros, *Wesley's World Parish*, 72.
2. Wesley, *Works of John Wesley*, 1:201–2.
3. Hardman, *Seasons of Refreshing*, 120.
4. Hardman, *Seasons of Refreshing*, 120.

and strength through the trials he underwent is available to needy people today. Yes, the church has the only message that can help those that are emotionally broken. The church should never be ashamed of what it has to offer. Repeatedly it has been proven that modern psychology and sociology have not been able to fix the problems of society; but where the gospel of Christ is offered, those who follow the Savior discover that he is able to help take the broken pieces of their life and put them all back together. However, it takes more than a cheap, easy type of religion; it takes a complete giving of control of a person's life to God.

REVIVING THE DEAD WITHIN THE CHURCH

A second scriptural principle is the necessity of taking the message of repentance first to the unsaved church members of our day. Paul took the message "to the Jew first, and also to the Greek" (Rom 1:16). Jesus, in his ministry, stated, "I am not sent but unto the lost sheep of the house of Israel" (Matt 15:24). The scriptural principle established both by Jesus and Paul is that those who should first be evangelized are those who already have Scripture, namely those who already have and believe the Bible but are not living according to the word of God. All churches do not teach a salvation message. The question is whether a person is saved. It is a person's fruit that identifies one as a Christian or not (Matt 7:15–20). The apostle John stated, "And hereby we do know that we know him [Christ], if we keep his commandments. He that saith, 'I know him,' and keepeth not his commandments, is a liar, and the truth is not in him" (1 John 2:3). If a person is not born again and living in accordance with God's commands, he is not a Christian and should be evangelized. Christ, our great example, began his ministry by calling the Jews to repentance (Matt 4:17). If a person is a follower of Christ, he should mimic Jesus by following his style of ministry and calling America's church to repentance. This is not a popular concept, but there are no other answers. The American church is dying and must radically change back to a biblical methodology or it will be the end for the American church. We must admit the problem and begin looking back to the Bible for answers.

ABSOLUTENESS OF BIBLICAL TRUTH

American culture today views intolerance as the worst form of behavior.[5] In the church this concept is often called judging. The idea of saying someone

---

5. McDowell and Hostetler, *New Tolerance*, 43–44.

of another religion is lost is completely anathema to our culture today. It causes great controversy anytime a denomination states that Catholics or Jews need to be saved; yet, that has been the Protestant belief from the beginning. The truth is still the truth whether it is popular in our culture or not. People are lost and in need of salvation whether it is "judging" to say so or not. Christians must follow the truth of the Bible and not be guided by contemporary postmodernism which does not accept absolute truth. Jesus, our great example, was quick to condemn the Pharisees for having "made the commandment of God of none effect" (Matt 15:6). Jesus also stated that the father of the Jewish leaders was the devil; and he compared them to beautifully painted tombs when he said, "Woe unto you, scribes and Pharisees, hypocrites! For ye are like unto whited sepulchers" (John 8:44; Matt 23:27). The apostles in the Scripture followed the same pattern and vehemently condemned sin, such as calling a leading church woman in Thyatira by the name Jezebel. A person should be very careful not to wrongfully judge others, and give each person the benefit of the doubt. God is the judge and not us; however, the church has failed "if thou dost not speak to warn the wicked from his way" (Ezek 33:8) If people are not warned, God said, "That wicked man shall die in his iniquity; but his blood will I require at thine hand" (Ezek 33:8). It is our responsibility to warn those who are lost no matter whether they profess to be a Christian or not. They must be identified and evangelized.

> The Bible is still the word of God and contains the absolute truth needed for salvation.

People who accept the postmodern concepts of today do not believe in absolute truth; yet, genuine Christians still do. The Bible is still the word of God and contains the absolute truth needed for salvation. Anyone who tries to find salvation outside of God's word will not. Most evangelical Christians will agree with this biblical stand, but will refuse to apply the truth that many who call themselves Christians are not. To be a Christian, a person must be born again and live a life that keeps God's commands. At the judgment Jesus will state to those who profess but do not know Christ, "I never knew you: depart from me, ye that work iniquity" (Matt 7:23). It is the job of the church to restore these lost souls to the Lord. Many of the great movements of history began with calling a sinful church to repentance, just as Jesus did. It was the message of Martin Luther, George Whitefield, John Wesley, the Puritans, and the Holiness movement. Their goal was to purify the church of the sin within it. Protestant Christianity has never accepted the idea that

Christians can and do constantly wilfully sin and live in rebellion to God until recently. Many, if not most, theological belief systems today have abandoned a biblical lifestyle.

COMPROMISE OF THE CALVINISTS

What has happened to those who follow the theology of John Calvin? The power and purity of those early Calvinists impacted much of Europe for Christ. Their revival swept across Europe and along with the Lutherans almost took all of Northern Europe for God. Yet today, the heirs of Calvinism often practice a cheap experience of salvation that does not transform the life of a believer. They then teach that it does not matter what a person does; he or she is eternally saved. This certainly was not the belief or practice of the early Calvinists or the Particular Baptists that accepted Calvin's ideas of election. Early Calvinists emphasized that if a person was one of the elect, God converted him, and that transformation was evidenced by the holy life they lived. John Calvin, in his commentary over 1 John 3:8–10, stated:

> The hearts of the godly are so effectually governed by the Spirit of God, that through an inflexible disposition they follow his guidance. . . . The power of the Spirit is so effectual, that it necessarily retains us in continual obedience to righteousness. . . . John declares that all who do not live righteously are not of God, because all those whom God calls, he regenerates by his Spirit. Hence newness of life is a perpetual evidence of divine adoption.[6]

Calvinists at one time were some of the most godly people that have lived in history. Calvin would agree that those who do not show evidence of the regenerating power of the Spirit of God are obviously not part of the elect or saved.

Those who are followers of Wesley and the Methodist heritage have done little better. Many of the Methodists and some holiness groups are now even questioning whether the Bible is the inerrant word of God. The Methodist Church at one time emphasized a born-again experience that changed lives. Yet now, the denomination, as are many with a Calvinistic heritage, is in the process of accepting such sins as gay marriage. Others with a Methodist background, including many within the Holiness movement, live a life which differs little from the culture around them.

---

6. Calvin, *Calvin's Commentary on the Bible*, I John 3:8–11.

Other evangelical groups have emphasized emotional services with contemporary music. This would be true of charismatic-style churches and many Pentecostal groups. The goal of the service is to help the people feel spiritual. Some people in praise-type worship services are excited about their relationship with God while yet living in blatant sin. Yet the Bible has little to say about feeling, instead emphasizing faith and righteousness. According to Scripture people who commit adultery, fornication, or are homosexuals, thieves, or drunkards shall not inherit the kingdom of God (1 Cor 6:9–10; Gal 5:19–21; Eph 5:5; Rev 21:8). The commands of God are being ignored by many churches in American society today; yet attendees feel good about their spiritual condition. There have been other times in history in which the church had only a few truly converted people left. America is like that today. In the past, God has often moved ministers to call the church to repentance. It will only be when the church repents that revival will occur. Scripture says, "If my people, which are called by my name, shall humble themselves, and pray, and seek my face, and turn from their wicked ways; then will I hear from heaven, and will forgive their sin, and will heal their land" (2 Chr 7:14). America's desperate need is to humbly turn to God for forgiveness and to forsake sin.

Those who believe the Scripture should be first evangelized because they already have a foundation of truth. Paul first went to the Jews, and normally there was a nucleus of Jewish people who believed. These people laid the foundation for the outreach to the gentiles. Christ and the apostles first went to the Jews, although there were many gentiles which were later converted. During the days of the apostles, the church was predominantly a Jewish group.

Any genuine Christian should appreciate being called to model their life more like Christ. Every Christian's desire is to become more Christlike. First John 3:3 says, "And every man that hath this hope in him purifieth himself." Anyone who fights against the truth does not have the Spirit of truth in him and does not know God. Although he or she may profess salvation, it is evident from their lack of interest that they have never been saved or have lost interest in God.

The sinners in our world will not be ready to listen unless the hypocritical church is first called to repent. Being identified as a Christian is not necessarily the best testimony in this age. The people of the world know those who profess to be Christians who lie, cheat, commit adultery, and listen to the same filthy stories as do the non-Christians. Much of society does not believe Christians are any different. In fact, Christians sometimes preach that they are no different either; they say they sin like everyone else, but are forgiven. One scholar stated, "These carnal Corinthians lived like unsaved men. That clarifies why the word 'carnal' can label both unbelievers and believers, simply because the lifestyles of both are the same."[7] It is no wonder that those in the world give the church little respect. Only when the church is called to repentance will the unconverted outside of the church be willing to listen to the message of the church. This is the biblical example.

Theodore Frelinghuysen gives a great example of the need to first call the church to repentance. He is the forerunner of the Great Awakening in colonial America. Upon arrival at his pastorate near Raritan, New Jersey, Frelinghuysen found that "religion consisted as the mere formal pursuit of the routine of duty," and regarded many of his members as "unsaved, pharisaical, and self-righteous."[8] He condemned their horse racing, gambling, and dissipation.[9] Although facing opposition within the ranks of the church, the people who lived in the area began to attend and a number were converted. It is believed his work laid the groundwork for the great revivals under George Whitefield and Gilbert Tennent.[10]

---

7. Ryrie, *So Great Salvation*, 62.
8. Hardman, *Seasons of Refreshing*, 54.
9. Hardman, *Seasons of Refreshing*, 54.
10. Hardman, *Seasons of Refreshing*, 60.

CHAPTER 10

Evangelism in a Postmodern World

Society has undergone a transformation since the mid-1900s. It seems almost nothing is the same. Churches previously used revival meetings as evangelistic tools. The church was often the most exciting show in town. Visitors thronged revival meetings, and the evangelist was often a professional who knew just how to expound the truth to convict the people of their sins and then present the gospel message to convert people.[1] It was effective, especially with the involvement of the local congregation who prayed, invited, shouted "amen," and emotionally were involved. Times have changed. Visitors seldom come to revival services, and other forms of entertainment have seized the imagination of the American public. The church is also far different. The emotional enthusiasm of the church has dissipated. Far too often the spiritual fervency is gone from the church. The excitement of the crowd and the power of God are gone, and often even church members no longer attend revival services. Accordingly, few churches have revivals today; and if they do, the length of the time has shortened from two weeks to just a few days.

Entertainment has changed; worldviews have changed; and there is a rising hostility in culture toward the church. We live in a different world; however, let us never forget the gospel has not changed. It still has the power to mend broken lives and still is a must for a person to go to heaven. No, the truth has not changed; and furthermore, God has not changed. He still is our omnipotent, omnipresent, omniscient Father. He knew beforehand of the challenges of this day. Our job is to discover how we can be part of God's plan for this age. He will continue to build his church.

---

1. Black and Drury, *Story of the Wesleyan Church*, 158.

IMPORTANCE OF ABSOLUTES

The emphasis of the church has shifted to becoming more relevant in our world rather than an emphasis upon the absolute standards of God's word. The goal would be quite laudable if it did not undermine the Scriptures. Many church leaders believe in order to reach our culture where it is, the church should have as few cultural barriers as possible. These leaders emphasize 1 Corinthians 9:19, which says, "I am made all things to all men, that I might by all means save some." They have a valid point. Scripture needs to be seen as relevant to our day. The culture of America today is not what it was in 1950 or even twenty years ago. Evangelistic methods that worked in the past may no longer be effective today. In order for the gospel to impact modern America, it must relate to the culture of today. Some things can be changed which are not absolutes in the Bible, and sometimes certain practices have a negative cultural connotation with which no Christian should want to be identified. Cultural meanings do change. In the early 1900s, the color red was sometimes identified with prostitution, and a person wearing that color was identified as an immoral person. At that time in some places the color should not have been worn, but that cultural understanding is long gone. There would be no value to still preach opposition to something that outdated. Often, in the desire to be more relevant, however, critical biblical values are being undermined. Any absolute which is based upon the word of God is not negotiable and cannot be compromised without threatening the gospel. The absolutes of God must be the first priority.

Underlying everything in evangelism is the concept of how people are saved. Are people primarily saved because God convicts them of sin and draws them to himself? Or are people saved because they choose to become a Christian? Most theologians today would agree that both concepts are true, but in which concept does the priority lie? Should the church focus upon doing what is necessary to please God and bring his power into the church, or should the church focus upon not offending people so they can more easily identify as a Christian? Current evangelistic thought usually gives lip service to pleasing Christ while focusing upon being culturally accommodating to the sinful world. Previous generations of Christians focused upon the power of the gospel to convict of sin as a necessary prerequisite to a person's choice. Scripture is clear that "No man can come to me [Jesus] except the Father which hath sent me draw him" (John 6:44). The theological revision in America which has downplayed the severity of sin has caused the change. After all, if God expects Christians to willfully sin, and this behavior in the church is not a major problem with God, why not please people; accordingly, the church has become more interested in being culturally relevant than in pleasing God. Current teaching in many churches does not insist that Christians continually practicing sin will hinder God moving in the conversion of sinners; yet the Bible says, "Your iniquities have separated between you and your God, and your sins have hid his face from you, that he will not hear" (Isa 59:2). It is no wonder the church today has no power. God is not listening to their prayers. Yet, God wants to lift people out of sin. Having the approval of God and pleasing him is far more important in lasting growth than in trying to do what pleases people.

BIBLICAL BASIS FOR ABSOLUTISM

What is the example of Christ and the apostles? Did they try to change the truth to make it more popular? They never tried to change the truth of God to make it popular. In fact, the opposite seems true. Jesus so angered the religious leaders that he was crucified. The message of the apostles often outraged the public. The most antagonistic statement that could be made to the Jewish people was to accuse them of murdering their Messiah. Yet, that was the message of Peter and the apostles at Pentecost. The early church so angered the leaders and the multitude that Stephen and James were executed. Paul caused a riot in almost every town he visited. The gospel was never softened in order to be sensitive to the seekers. Furthermore, these people who were so offensive are held up as biblical examples for us to follow. It was obviously not a culturally acceptable message that was preached. Instead the accusation was that they "have turned the world upside down" (Acts 17:6).

The basic goal of the church should be to change an individual to one whose character is controlled by a desire to be like Christ. "It is God's life-changing power that is able to touch every individual, who then has the responsibility to touch the world around him with the absolutes found in the Bible."[2] There should be little desire to fit in with the world, but a drive to live holy in this present world. Scripture teaches that a person should not be "conformed to this world: but be ye transformed by the renewing of your mind" (Rom 12:2). Unfortunately, much modern evangelism is driven by a desire to conform to the world in order to identify with and attract sinners. The goal seems to be to remove any possible difference between Christian culture and the culture of the world so as to not impede evangelism. This has led to a continual lowering of the Christian lifestyle until it is difficult to distinguish the behavior, music, dress styles, and entertainment of "Christians" from that of the sinful society around us. "Evangelicals have, with tragic results, accommodated to the world spirit of this age. This has to do with the

---

2. Schaeffer, *Great Evangelical Disaster*, 40.

whole area of marriage, family, sexual morality, feminism, homosexuality, and divorce."[3] Any evangelism that leads to a cheap religion will always lead to a lowering of God's requirements in order to not offend people.

The type of evangelism that does not confront sin is also clearly unbiblical. Christ and the disciples were bold and direct in their confrontation of sin. Christ and the apostles demanded repentance. Speaking to the pagan philosophers on Mars Hill, Paul stated that God now "commandeth all men everywhere to repent" (Acts 17:30). He did not lower Christianity to make it palatable to the Greek culture; instead, he demanded the Greeks admit they were wrong and then change. The passage which is commonly used to defend the practice of lowering scriptural standards and not confronting sin is 1 Corinthians 9:19–23, where Paul discussed how he identified with Jews, the gentiles, and the weak. He stated that he was "made all things to all men, that I might by all means save some." Yet, this passage does not teach any lowering of Christian behavior; it only advocates identifying and working in different cultural settings as would any missionary. Our goal in evangelism, whether in foreign missions or in our own country, is not to Americanize but to Christianize. However, much of modern evangelism has so diluted the gospel that it is failing to produce genuine Christians. As Francis Schaeffer said, "What is the use of evangelicalism seeming to get larger and larger if sufficient numbers of those under the name evangelical no longer hold to that which makes evangelicalism evangelical?"[4]

COSTS OF COMPROMISE

While it is quite evident evangelism that focuses upon being contemporary will undermine biblical standards, it is often missed that this type of evangelism also destroys long-term growth. In order to attract a sinful world, the church must have something different to offer. Denominations which grow consistently have a reason to exist. They proclaim that reason, and they emphasize it as their purpose for existence. It is possible for a local church, under the leadership of a dynamic pastor and an effective program, to build a large church by compromising the gospel; but it is not possible to replicate that pattern throughout a denomination. Furthermore, even if it were possible to build a denomination upon this basis, it would be built upon a shaky foundation that could not survive. Shallow, superficial Christianity (if there is such a thing) can sometimes attract a multitude of those who are looking for a less costly religion; however, they themselves do not

3. Schaeffer, *Great Evangelical Disaster*, 130.
4. Schaeffer, *Great Evangelical Disaster*, 64.

have the level of commitment which is necessary for the long-term success of the church. Their children will even be less committed and will abandon the church as is happening at the present. Many communities are packed with the children of evangelicals who claim to be saved but no longer see any purpose in church attendance. According to George Barna, "A large majority of the nation's unchurched population is drawn from the sector comprised of people who consider themselves Christians."[5]

The more conservative denominations among the evangelicals will find that contemporary seeker-sensitive evangelism will not bring growth to their groups, even shallow growth. For example, pastors among conservative churches who try to attract those from outside their church by de-emphasizing their differences will find this does not work. New people will soon decide more liberal churches can provide all the benefits of going to heaven without the cost. In order to keep those who come, a church must emphasize their reason for existence and convince all new people that their beliefs are not only true but also necessary. Yes, many will reject and leave, but that does not mean they would have stayed anyway. Those who come must be convinced of the necessity of the doctrinal beliefs and behavioral customs of the church or they will be gone in due time anyway. Accordingly, the goal of the church is to try to determine the best procedure regarding how to have new people experience for themselves the truth of God in their heart and come to believe in the validity of that church's message.

A deemphasis of truth has another important negative, even if it is done in order to more successively evangelize. A doctrinal belief or practice that is being challenged by the culture must be continuously preached and emphasized or it will soon be lost by the people of that church. Initially, the group will continue to practice and keep the behavior but will no longer consider it important. After all, if a practice is important it would be preached. The next step occurs when many or most of the people no longer believe that guideline; however, because few wish to cause problems, they still keep a church's behavioral standard. At this point the church has lost the battle on the issue, but almost everyone still looks and acts the same. There is little discernible difference, but in reality that belief or practice is gone. Eventually, some who are more outspoken or are rebellious will test the issue and will not be challenged. Within a short period of time almost everyone changes their outward behavior or beliefs. Those who oppose the change are shocked by what has happened; but in reality, the battle has long been decided in the minds of the people—it was just not yet obvious.

---

5. Barna, *Future Cast*, 158.

A person I knew attended a church which did not believe that a person should wear a necktie. It was thought that this was a sign of worldliness; but they did recognize there were good people who felt differently, and they did use visiting ministers who did wear a necktie. Out of curiosity, one person in the church asked all of the young married men in the church how they felt about wearing ties. None of them personally felt that it was a problem, but they kept the rule so as not to offend others. He had difficulty finding anyone except one person who was opposed to the tie. Yet, all of them kept the standard. Within five years almost all of the men in the church, including the new minister, were wearing neckties. Opposition to a necktie is very far removed from the issues of our day, but the principles of change still remain.[6]

Any countercultural issue which is not fervently believed and continually defended as a necessity will soon be gone. This is especially true among young people and new converts, but it also affects older people. Doctrinal beliefs regarding biblical inerrancy, creation, eternal punishment, and absolute truth are being challenged in many churches. Practices such as social drinking, gambling, and gay marriage are rapidly being accepted by many evangelicals. Every church group today is faced with a battle over some behavioral guideline. All practices are not equally important. Some issues which relate more to past traditions may be outdated and are not that important, and other issues which relate to carefulness can vary in how the issue is approached. Some practices, however, go to the heart of a biblical command. Each person must determine what positions are worth the fight and then stand for their belief, or the battle on that issue will be lost. Church leaders must personally be thoroughly convinced of the importance of their beliefs, and these beliefs must then be continually repeated and defended to their people, their young, and to all newly evangelized converts. Clear scriptural principles cannot be for sale. To abandon biblical truth is to undermine the foundation of the church. Without a proper foundation which gives a clear-cut purpose, no marketing strategy or growth methodology can provide long-term numerical success.

> Without the Spirit's transforming power, the church becomes just another entertainment or social club.

Many modern techniques have provided excellent insights into attracting people to church and ensuring they keep coming back; however, the philosophy of changing the church to not be offensive to the world, rather

---

6. This was done by my older brother who was attending at that time a church which took this position. He shared with me the results of his survey.

than transforming the sinner to fit the presence of God, has undermined the gospel. Christianity is by nature a radical religion. It is the way of the cross. Cheap religion will not have the power of God to effect genuine conversion. Without the Spirit's transforming power, the church becomes just another entertainment or social club; and its numbers will decline as young people abandon religion as worthless.

CULTURAL CHANGE

Things have changed in our country dramatically since the 1960s. According to James White, most unchurched Americans a generation ago would have been comparatively easy to evangelize and convert. They would have accepted many of the key biblical doctrines such as the deity of Christ and a belief in the Bible as the word of God. They would have had "a positive image of the church and its leaders, a church background and experience that was relatively healthy . . . [and] a built-in sense of guilt or conviction that kicked in when he or she violated the basic tenets of the Judeo-Christian value system."[7] Any solid efforts made to evangelize were usually rewarded with results. In most ways America was based upon a Christian foundation. Little groundwork needed to be laid. The harvest was "ripe already to harvest" (John 4:35). "The top evangelistic strategies of 1960—revivals, door-to-door visitation, Sunday school, and busing—were well orientated to this context."[8] Parents wanted their children in church and encouraged them to attend, and the parents were also often converted. Ministers and Christians were respected and were welcomed as visitors in the home. Sinners commonly attended revivals and tent meetings because it was the culturally acceptable thing to do. Evangelists were expected to condemn sin and preach about hell. Often conviction followed the preaching, and many were converted; lives were changed, and churches were expanded or established.

Tragically, this is not the America of the mid-twentieth century. The ready acceptance of the gospel by the world has been overtaken by apathy. Parents simply do not care, and the church or ministry no longer carries the same level of respect they once held. Not only is evangelism faced with apathy, but there is also a rising antagonism toward Christians. Many people see Christians as intolerant bigots who are threats to society. Moreover, "the typical unchurched person is not simply unchurched, but . . . more than likely he or she is in the none category."[9] They are often without any reli-

7. White, *Rise of the Nones*, 90.
8. White, *Rise of the Nones*, 91.
9. White, *Rise of the Nones*, 91.

gion at all and question that religious truth even exists. They must first be convinced the Christian way is correct. Obviously, the same methodology that was successful in the past will only have a limited success today. In many instances churches have put in a great deal of labor but obtained only minimal success or none at all.

Postmodern philosophy that does not accept absolutes has impacted the church. Charles Colson discussed an evangelical church that decided to grow. A survey discovered that the word "Baptist" in the name was a negative for many people, so the name was changed to a more popular term. The church removed its religious symbols such as the cross. These symbols might make people feel uncomfortable. The pastor shifted his preaching to more popular and positive topics rather than emphasizing doctrines such as damnation and hell. Sure enough, the church grew. One member stated it this way: "There's a spirit of putting people over doctrine. The church totally accepts people as they are without any sort of don'ts and dos."[10] Too many other churches have followed this same pattern. Biblical absolutes have been exchanged for a feel-good religion. The moral authority of the Bible and Christian doctrine have been undermined by this philosophy. Not only will this church have shortly lost it biblical values, but in the long term the church will die numerically. It has lost its reason for existence. Even more tragically, a church which has followed this program will influence other churches and people to accept an unbiblical value system that will undermine the entire church world. This pattern has replicated itself across much of the American landscape. The church is beginning to reap the consequences of watering down truth to gain numbers, and wide cracks are appearing in the foundation of the American Christian church.

FELLOWSHIP EVANGELISM

It has commonly been stated that in order to win a convert you must first win them to yourselves and then win them to God. This is often how the most successful evangelism occurs today. People need to know someone cares; and if a person has the love of God in their heart, it will be natural to reach out to hurting people to comfort them. As Christians, we should always look for opportunities to build relationships in order to evangelize. Churches should plan services or other activities that will attract the relatives, friends, and neighbors of our church people. As the relationship builds between those people and the church, an opportunity often comes to win them to God. Once a person has become converted, it is very important

---

10. Veith, *Postmodern Times*, 213.

their friendships and social ties are with the church people. This social bonding as part of the family of God is needed because people are social beings. If this bond is broken, it is rare that a person stays true to God.

As important as fellowship in evangelism is, there are some dangers. Many of these dangers can be avoided if the Christian is straightforward and up-front about his beliefs. He should always take a clear stand for truth. One of these dangers is the friendship may lead a Christian away from the church. The sinner may draw the Christian back into sin instead of the Christian leading the sinner to Christ. Another problem is that truth may become a threat to the friendship. A person who is showing interest in the church does not need to have all their lifestyle condemned. They need to first become a Christian. Accordingly, standards are deemphasized in the hope of winning them to God. Thus, friendship evangelism can become a threat to the continued existence of truth. Fellowship with non-Christians for the sake of evangelism should be done on the basis of truth. A person must be clear about their motives and not try to trick people into becoming saved or part of the church. We must always be honest about the cost of serving Christ. Often when people are brought into the church without understanding the true cost of the gospel, they abandon the church or find another church that is compromising, and the final end is worse than before the attempts were made. Often the gospel has been compromised as a consequence of outreach. This was one of the major reasons why many in the Holiness movement changed their practices in the 1960s. The leaders a few years earlier decided to emphasize "evangelism rather than legalism," proclaiming that "rigid enforcement of rules would hinder evangelism."[11] It did not work. Not only did the Wesleyans and the Nazarenes lose much of the conservatism that had characterized the movement, their rate of growth also declined.

Fellowship evangelism was not practiced in the book of Acts. Social bonding of Christians occurred after conversion, not before. Paul generally was not in a locality long enough to become close friends with the sinners in the communities in which he ministered. Once they were converted, however, there was a close bond which developed between Paul and his converts. Paul stated that he cared for them "even as a nurse cherisheth her children . . . [and] were willing to have imparted unto you, not the gospel of God only, but also our own souls, because ye were dear unto us" (1 Thess 2:7–8).

---

11. Haines and Thomas, *Outline History of the Wesleyan Church*, 112. The concept is also found in Black, *Holiness Heritage*, 117–18.

ENTERTAINMENT-STYLE EVANGELISM

Many churches have turned to entertainment as the means of evangelism. The service becomes a concert in which a praise team performs for the audience. Emotion ripples across the audience as congregants stand and sway to the music. The sermon is a masterpiece of oratory delivered with a polished performance. There are constant activities to entertain and bring in people. Star performers are brought into the church to attract audiences. Activities such as ball games and dramatic programs are staples of the church program. Children are cared for and entertained by professionals. This is the American megachurch scene. Successful churches are packing out their buildings with thousands of attendees. Many Pentecostal churches which led the way in emotionally-centered worship-type services are growing. Yet, is it working? Is the modern methodology of entertainment and inciting emotion creating a more Christian country? What impact is it having upon the people? Are Christians living more holy lives, or has holiness of life been overlooked in the middle of a feel-good religion? It is obvious some places are growing and expanding, but is it a shallow, cheap Christianity that is hardly Christian? Is Christ the Lord of their lives, or are they just trying to accept him as Savior while living selfish lives?

The reality is this emotionally centered type of religion is producing warped Christians. Emotionally hyped, positive music and messages will lead attendees to feel good about themselves spiritually; but the heart and life may be totally corrupt, and the spiritual cancer is covered over. God wants to transform lives, but emotionally centered religion makes it all but impossible for God to break through the excitement and deal with the heart issues of life. These attendees are convinced they are right with God because they feel spiritual, but the core of Christianity is to live a life that objectively follows the example of Christ in all things. Christianity in previous days would not fit the current entertainment-minded, fun-driven American evangelical. The current church fits Paul's description of the last days, when people would be "lovers of pleasures more than lovers of God" (1 Tim 3:4).

The concept of entertainment has completely pervaded American society. Even the most conservative churches in their youth camps, bus ministries, and other church activities focus upon making sure everyone has a good time. Previously, the focus was upon making sure everything was done to the glory of God. Certainly, there is nothing wrong with making activities fun, and this must be done to some degree to bring in outsiders; but it has gained in priority far above its value. People have become selfish and choose churches based upon what they selfishly desire. The question should be: What does God want? Or, does the church preach, teach, and live the truth? No longer is it considered important to go where a person can be the greatest blessing. Increasingly, people feel that even attendance is no longer of importance. The attitude of Americans today is: if I do not feel like going, I do not go. According to George Barna, many Christians have dropped completely out of church to opt for other means of meeting with others and God.[12] Yet, Christ came to build his church (Matt 16:18). If a person is not part of the church, they are not part of what Christ came to build.

An entertainment-driven church strives to please sinful men rather than God. Their focus is upon doing whatever it takes in order to get people to attend; accordingly, the church pushes the edge on questionable moral activities. The music, programs, preaching, dress styles, etc. are all geared toward not offending the attendees that the church is trying to reach from the world. Yet, Jesus states, "without me ye can do nothing." The true church goes forward only in the power of the Holy Spirit. It may be possible for false religions to grow, but not the true church. It may even be possible to gather numbers of people, but are they truly converted if they have not become new creatures in Christ Jesus (2 Cor 5:17)? Predominantly, much of the American church world is building entertainment centers with a facade of religiosity. Jesus, however, taught that to bring forth fruit a person must abide in him (John 15:5). It is not possible to truly build the church without first focusing upon abiding in Christ and receiving his blessing.

---

12. Barna, *Future Cast*, 147.

CHAPTER 11

The Biblical Method of Growth—Part 1

The biblical method of growth is a fervent group of people who believe in the necessity of their belief. The people in the early church boldly and uncompromisingly filled their local communities with their doctrine about Jesus Christ through the power of the Holy Spirit.

1. CHRIST WAS PRESENTED AS THE LORD AND THE ONLY SAVIOR (ACTS 2:26; 5:30-31; 13:38).

The method of the early church was to present Christ as the only Lord and Savior. They taught that there was no "salvation in any other: for there is none other name under heaven given among men, whereby we must be saved" (Acts 4:12). Christianity is an exclusive religion. In order to be saved a person must believe in Jesus Christ. There are not different ways to God; there is only one way, and that is through Christ. Everyone else is going to hell. This concept is not popular in modern Western culture, but this has always been the position of the church. Those in Acts who were converted then became part of the fellowship of believers. For a biblical church body to grow, these beliefs are absolutely necessary.

The mainline churches of today who no longer believe or emphasize that Christ is the only way to heaven are all collapsing in attendance. Evangelical churches had rapid growth rates during the twentieth century but now are following the mainline churches in the pattern of decline. According to Dean Kelley, the decline of the traditional American churches such as the Episcopal Church, the Methodist Church, the Lutheran Church, and the Presbyterian

Church is due to the ecumenical nature of their religion. He identified that the loss of absolutism about distinctive doctrines led to a weakened concept regarding the necessity of a group's doctrinal beliefs. A church's leniency in enforcing penalties against those who deviated from the accepted practices of a group undermined the distinctives of their lifestyle. He also emphasized that an appreciative view of outsiders rather than being critical regarding differing beliefs and practices were key factors which led to the numerical losses of mainline churches.[1] It is difficult for a denomination to grow unless the reasons for its existence are clearly understood and emphasized.

The evangelical church world has now followed the same pattern. No longer do they outspokenly condemn the world as lost and headed for judgment. Evangelicals have conformed to a lifestyle that is more acceptable to society and have moderated their distinctives to a few practices which identify a person as a Christian. Evangelical theology has been weakened by a failure to emphasize the justice of God along with his love. Christianity has become a feel-good religion with no penalty for sin. A rising standard of living along with an ecumenical spirit from working with others in politics or higher education has undermined the absolutism of the church. No longer does the church have the dynamics of a burning message which demands identification with a radical group as a necessity for salvation. Evangelicals have become a respected part of society and are quite satisfied with this world. It is no wonder there is a struggle for growth. Many evangelical churches have lost the purpose for their existence since to them salvation has become only a cheap acceptance of Christ as Savior. In addition, the eternal security belief as now taught means church attendance is optional. Some denominations and churches have seen their foundations eroded by the acceptance of the doctrine of evolution which has undermined the belief in the inerrancy of Scripture. The denominations which are showing the most growth today are those who are quite different from the culture and unbending in their beliefs and practices.

2. A BOLD CONDEMNATION OF HYPOCRITICAL RELIGION AND A DEMAND FOR REPENTANCE (ACTS 2:38; 17:38)

The biblical pattern has always been to boldly condemn sin. Does it make people angry? Yes. John the Baptist and Jesus were both executed for their messages condemning the practices of their day. This pattern followed

---

1. Kelley, *Why Conservative Churches Are Growing*, 84.

throughout history. Those who have built a large following that lasted did so by condemning the evils of their day and presenting the grace of God which has the power to deliver. Most people will be offended and will turn away from the message, but there will be a small minority that will repent and become part of the group. This minority, however, will be committed to the cause. Over time this small but steady increase continues to build the denomination.

> A small but zealous band of evangelistically minded true believers has more lasting impact than a larger uncommitted group.

Movements grow in the long term not by the inclusion of a great number of marginally committed people but by focusing upon bringing deeply committed people into the belief system. This was the method of Jesus Christ. He was fervently evangelistic in spreading the truth, but he also drove the multitudes away by his strong, almost fanatical, message. Christ's focus was upon building a small but firmly committed set of disciples (John 6:53–60). A small but zealous band of evangelistically minded true believers has more lasting impact, not only in spreading truth but also in preserving it, than a larger uncommitted group. When God moves in revival power, this small, fervent band may suddenly explode into almost overwhelming numbers. Not only did this occur in Acts 2, but this explosive pattern has occurred down throughout history. America has experienced this explosive growth in both of the Great Awakenings.

The goal of boldly condemning sin is to bring conviction upon the hearer. This was the pattern in the Methodist Church. They were to "Preach as if you had seen heaven and its celestial inhabitants, and had hovered over the bottomless pit and beheld the tortures and heard the groans of the damned."[2] "Not only did they publicly preach with effectiveness, they privately and capably reproved sin—face to face. . . . [and] many were brought to conviction by the faithful rebukes of the Methodists."[3] Truth must be proclaimed boldly and scripturally in the marketplace of ideas with the goal of convicting and convincing others of its validity.

John the Baptist confronted the Pharisees and Sadducees, proclaiming, "O generation of vipers, who hath warned you to flee from the wrath to come? Bring forth therefore fruits meet for repentance" (Matt 3:7–8). Jesus confronted those of his day, crying out, "Woe unto you, scribes and Pharisees, hypocrites! For ye compass sea and land to make one proselyte, and when he is made, ye make him twofold more the child of hell than

---

2. Atnip, *How the Methodists Saved America*, 108.
3. Atnip, *How the Methodists Saved America*, 115.

yourselves" (Matt 23:15). Peter in his preaching to the people after the healing of the lame man told the multitude, "Ye . . . killed the Prince of life, whom God hath raised from the dead" (Acts 3:15). Nothing could have been more offensive to the Jewish people than to accuse them of killing their Messiah. Stephen followed the same concept when standing before the Sanhedrin, saying, "Ye stiffnecked and uncircumcised in heart and ears, ye do always resist the Holy Ghost: as your fathers did, so do ye . . . and they have slain them which shewed before of the coming of the Just One of whom ye have been now the betrayers and murderers (Acts 7:51–52). In the face of persecution, the apostles in Jerusalem prayed to God to "grant unto thy servants, that with all boldness they may speak thy word" (Acts 4:29). Paul in his ministry caused a riot in almost every town he visited and asked the church to pray that "I may open my mouth boldly, to make known the mystery of the gospel" (Eph 6:19).

Boldness should not come from a confrontational nature but from a deep-seated desire and love for the truth and for the souls of those with whom a person meets. Lost people have a right to straightforward truth. There is no reason to try to deceive them about the cost of the gospel. A person should always work at presenting the most positive and defensible aspects of truth surrounded by Christian love and prayer. In fact, if the love of God is not in one's heart and fervent prayer has not been made to God, it is better to keep quiet rather than to speak in such a way that would drive people away from God. Yet, people must have the truth even if they choose to turn away. Scripture says when Christ was talking to the rich young ruler, he "loved him, and said unto him, 'One thing thou lackest: go thy way, sell whatsoever thou hast, and give to the poor, and thou shalt have treasure in heaven: and come, take up the cross, and follow me.' And he was sad at that saying, and went away grieved" (Mark 10:21–22). Jesus stated the very words that drove that man away, but it came from a heart full of love and honesty. This same attitude is what the church needs today.

The basic message of the Bible is the necessity of teaching all people that they are lost and in need of salvation. To accomplish this it takes a straightforward condemnation of the sins of society, and for the church to explain their lost condition. The message must also be repeated until the hearers are either converted or angered. The three possible reactions to the gospel are acceptance of the truth, anger and rejection of the truth, or apathy and a careless attitude toward truth. Most people currently react with apathy since they are untouched by the gospel and unconvicted.

3. THE NEED FOR THE FILLING OF THE SPIRIT

Christ and the early church emphasized the need for the filling of the Spirit. Jesus commanded the disciples "that they should not depart from Jerusalem, but wait for the promise of the Father. . . . For John truly baptized with water; but ye shall be baptized with the Holy Ghost not many days hence" (Acts 1:4). The true church can only go forward under the power of the Spirit of God. The apostles constantly preached that the church can and must be filled with the Spirit. Peter promised the crowd at Pentecost, "Ye shall receive the gift of the Holy Ghost" (Acts 2:28). Peter and John were sent to believers in Samaria since the Spirit had as of yet "fallen upon none of them" (Acts 8:16). Paul asked the believers at Ephesus, "Have ye received the Holy Ghost since ye believed?" (Acts 19:2). Being filled with the Spirit was a major focus of the ministry and preaching of the early church.

4. THE GREAT COMMISSION— EVANGELIZATION AND EDIFICATION

The first responsibility of the church, according to the Great Commission, is to evangelize the unsaved. Its command is to, "Go ye into all the world, and preach the gospel (Mark 16:15). The meaning of the word "gospel" is good news. Salvation is certainly good news to a lost world. The church has the responsibility to proclaim this message to every corner of the globe and to all people. Those who believe in Christ and are willing to publicly identify with the Christian message will be saved. The church's job is to spread the message. Each pastor certainly wants success, but our call is to be faithful. Christ is to be presented with the message of the gospel that takes away sin. Paul stated, "For Christ sent me not to baptize, but to preach the gospel. . . . For I determined not to know any thing among you, save Jesus Christ, and him crucified" (1 Cor 1:17; 2:2).

The second responsibility of the church according to the Great Commission is the edification and discipling of converts. "Teaching them to observe all things whatsoever I have commanded you" (Matt 28:20). Namely it was expected that the church would teach new converts to behave like a Christian, and it was expected that the converts would adopt the lifestyle of the church. It was expected for new converts to look to their leaders for proper behavior. Paul stated, "Be ye followers of me, even as I also am of Christ," (1 Cor 11:1) and, "Wherefore, my beloved, as ye have always obeyed, not as in my presence only, but now much more in my absence," (Phil 2:12) and, "Brethren, be followers together of me, and mark them which walk so as ye have us for an example," (Phil 3:17) and finally, "For yourselves know how ye ought to follow us: for we behaved not ourselves disorderly among you" (2 Thess 3:7).

External behavioral guidelines in such things as dress and entertainment are not the core of the gospel—a heart transformation is. However, it was anticipated that all of those who were Christians should live the lifestyle that the disciples exemplified. No church should downplay the cost of the gospel. If a person becomes a Christian, they should know this is expected of them. Many of the differences in lifestyle are quite obvious to new people or to those outside the church. These practices should be readily defended. Sometimes a guideline can be defended by simply stating it is done because a person believes that is what God asks them to do. To undermine a standard by not defending it will soon cause the individual or church to lose that belief. Behavioral guidelines do hinder some people from becoming part of a church, but the greatest difficulty occurs when a group has practices which they are unwilling to defend. Being more strict helps a denomination to grow, but this is only true if the people boldly articulate the necessity of their stigmata.[4]

5. TWO EVANGELISTIC STYLES GIVEN IN JUDE—COMPASSION AND FEAR OF SIN

The book of Jude gives two different styles of evangelism, one with an emphasis upon love and the other upon condemnation of sin. "Some have compassion, making a difference, and others save with fear . . . hating even the garment spotted by the flesh" (Jude 22–23). Often those of one style condemn the other type of message. When the emphasis of one evangelist is upon the love of Christ, he commonly downplays or even opposes preaching that emphasizes fear and denouncing sin. Those who denounce sin often feel that emphasizing love is not the best way to reach people; they need to be confronted with their guilt. In reality, God uses both types of evangelists. It depends upon the need of the individual. A person who is broken by sin and in despair needs to know God cares, but one who is lost yet blind with false confidence needs to be confronted with their personal guilt before God. Both the love and the justice of God need to be emphasized. The failure to preach both sides of the truth will lead toward an imbalance in the message and will undermine the effectiveness of evangelism. It takes both the positive and the negative for the outreach of the gospel to be effective.

---

4. Kelley, *Why Conservative Churches Are Growing*, 95.

Our culture has veered too far in not emphasizing the justice of God. God's love does need to be preached and cannot be overemphasized, but failure to preach against sin and warning about the judgment has given us a world in which seemingly no one fears God. Some professing Christians believe it does not matter if they deliberately disobey God; neither do they feel it is necessary to go to church. In fact, they do whatever they want to do and are confident they are still Christians. According to the theology of our culture, being a Christian has nothing to do with what a person does or currently believes. Society has abandoned the belief in a literal hell where those who reject God will be punished. Even Christian scholars have begun denying this truth of the Bible, feeling that "the biblical language about fire and flames is figurative."[5] Yet, nothing could be clearer in the Bible. Those who reject God "shall go away into everlasting punishment: but the righteous into life eternal" (Matt 25:46). The only person who came from eternity to earth was Jesus Christ. He knew what the souls of people were facing in the future. The teaching of Jesus repeatedly warned about the dangers of hell and the judgment. If our ministry parallels the ministry of our great example, a person should preach the same topics which Christ preached. A minister should also emphasize the same priorities as Christ. Warnings about death, hell, or the judgment was one of Jesus's major themes in his teaching.

Genuine love and compassion are desperately needed in our society today. As our culture becomes more and more ungodly, a greater number of people with broken lives will be desperately looking for hope. Through Christ, the church has the only answer to meet the emotional needs of our hurting world. It is not condemnation these people need for their sin; they are looking for love and hope. This is something the church can provide. These people already know the consequences of their sin. Jesus reached out to many sinners in this category, such as the woman who was accused of adultery and brought before Jesus. The religious leaders brought the woman to Jesus asking for him to condemn her. The woman knew the penalty of the law was stoning; but instead of being harsh and judgmental, Jesus reached out in love to the woman. His actions caused the accusers to leave; and then he spoke words of forgiveness, saying, "Neither do I condemn thee: go, and sin no more" (John 8:11). He did not criticize, but rather forgave, and then demanded a change in her life. Repentant, needy people in our communities need compassionate evangelism.

It was love that caused God to send his Son to pay the price for our sins. It was love that held Jesus Christ to the cross, not the nails. Anyone

---

5. Strobel, *Case for Faith*, 248.

who is filled with the Spirit will have the nature of God inside of them. God's nature is holy and just but also merciful and loving. When Jesus saw the multitudes, "he was moved with compassion on them" (Matt 9:36). Paul said of his ministry at Thessalonica, "We were gentle among you, even as a nurse cherisheth her children" (1 Thess 2:7). "Most people will not care how much you know until they know how much you care."[6] No matter how strongly and fervently one preaches and stands for truth, if we are to be like Christ it must be evident that we love and care for other people. Our goal is not to condemn but to lead people to Christ. As Christ would not break a bruised reed nor quench a smoking flax (Matt 12:20), we must go to any possible length to encourage any person who makes a move toward God.

The apostle John gave two characteristics which identify the children of God. He said, "In this the children of God are manifest, and the children of the devil: whosoever doeth not righteousness is not of God, neither he that loveth not his brother. For this is the message that ye heard from the beginning, that we should love one another. We know that we have passed from death unto life, because we love the brethren. He that loveth not his brother abideth in death" (1 John 3:10–11, 14). The key for both types of evangelism is to pray until God breaks our heart with love for the one to whom we are witnessing. Only then can a person have the wisdom to reach out to another as needed in their life. Certainly, a harsh and critical spirit is always damaging to the cause of Christ, but the opposite is likewise true: compromising truth in order to not offend will destroy the very power of the gospel and undermine the absolutes of the Bible.

---

6. Theodore Roosevelt, https://www.brainyquote.com/quotes/theodore_roosevelt_140484.

CHAPTER 12

The Biblical Method of Growth—Part 2

When any biblical key is lacking, it is much more difficult for the church to go forward. In modern America many of the New Testament ingredients for church growth are absent. It is no wonder that often great effort only brings minimal results. Church growth has become the major rallying cry of our day. Churches often have a singular focus upon growth; yet, no matter how hard the churches of our day work, it seems there is little long-lasting success. These poor results are true of denominations from mainstream churches to evangelical groups and even to very conservative denominations. Each of these groups needs to go back to the Bible for the scriptural pattern of growth.

6. VIEWING OTHERS AS LOST

The church in the book of Acts viewed their world as lost and in need of the gospel. When speaking to the Jewish leaders, Peter stated, "Neither is there salvation in any other: for there is none other name under heaven given among men, whereby we must be saved" (Acts 4:12). He insisted the Jewish religious leaders and people along with all other men were lost and unsaved unless they believed in Christ. Paul likewise, in speaking to the philosophers at Athens, said God "now commandeth all men every where to repent: Because he hath appointed a day, in the which he will judge the world" (Acts 17:30–31). The message of the early church was clear: either become a Christian or you are lost. The church clearly understood its reason for existence. The world was lost and hell-bound. The church's job was to save souls by announcing the good news of salvation.

> When a church member has no evidence of a converted life, nor do they show the fruits of being a Christian, are they actually saved (Matt 7:16–18)?

This same exclusiveness is gone from the church world of our day. Few people in our world would consider themselves as lost and in danger of going to hell. Mainline churches now see Christianity as only one of the paths to God. Doctrines such as hell and the judgment are no longer emphasized, and the world no longer believes these basic truths. Even some Bible-believing churches question whether a good, loving God would send or allow people to be cast into eternal punishment. Evangelicals have replaced genuine repentance and faith in Christ that comes from the heart as the means of salvation with a few steps that mentally attest that Christ is God. Some insist no repentance or change of life is necessary. They insist Christ can be taken as Savior without taking him as Lord. Furthermore, many insist that since salvation is by faith, it does not matter what a person does after going through their cheap salvation formula; they believe a person is eternally secure and cannot be lost. These evangelicals would consider as Christians some who are currently atheists, immoral, or even mass murderers, as long as those individuals had prayed the sinner's prayer at some point in their lives. According to their belief regarding eternal security, church attendance is superfluous to salvation; therefore there is no need for a person to attend church, thus undermining church attendance. A large majority of people in America consider themselves Christians. Many of those who were raised in the church but are not currently attending have at some point in time professed to be born again. But are they actually born again? Does not the Bible teach that "if any man be in Christ, he is a new creature: old things are passed away; behold, all things are become new" (2 Cor 5:17)? When a person has no evidence of a converted life, nor do they show the fruits of being a Christian, are they actually saved (Matt 7:16–18)? No longer does the modern church follow the New Testament concept that those outside of the church are lost sinners. Until those who no longer attend church or who do not live a biblical lifestyle are considered sinners in need of conversion, it will become increasingly impossible for the church to effectively evangelize, attract new converts, and build the church numerically.

One of the major factors undermining the belief regarding the necessity of church attendance is the way the doctrine of eternal security has been modified. The original belief of Reformed theology was that if a person was saved he or she would persevere to the end, and a failure to live a Christian life was evidence a person had never been saved. Now it is taught that if a person is saved, he should live a Christian life; but if not, he can never lose his salvation no matter how sinful his behavior—thus any and all sins are excused. This new twist of the doctrines regarding grace and eternal security has infiltrated all of Christendom, but it is in conflict with historic Christian beliefs. John Calvin emphasized predestination, which means God chooses those who will be saved and those who will be damned. All that is left of Calvin's concept of predestination for many, if not most, of the Calvinists is a distorted view of his doctrine of the perseverance of the saints. "With Calvin, holiness of life was the proof that one was among the elect, but today's semi-Calvinism believes that neither sin nor holiness affect the final destiny of one who has ever trusted Christ as his Savior."[1]

The ultimate effect of this doctrine is that church attendance and moral behavior have become detached from salvation. It seems almost everyone in America today believes they are going to heaven no matter how they live. Furthermore, the church often agrees with them, if at any time that person prayed the sinner's prayer. For this reason, the church is often more effective in pagan countries than in America. In non-Christian countries the church views those around them as lost and in need of the gospel, while in America many who live like pagans profess to have been born again. Christianity has been degraded to the point where church attendance and morality are optional. It is true that salvation only takes a simple prayer, provided it is from the heart; but the evidence of regeneration will be shown by the life which follows.

> Christianity has been degraded to the point where church attendance and morality are optional.

7. AGGRESSIVE DOCTRINAL EVANGELISM

The leaders of the Jewish Council told the early church, "Ye have filled Jerusalem with your doctrine" (Acts 5:28). Later, the early church openly battled intellectually on both theological and philosophical lines in the Greco-Roman Empire. Other successful groups have always emphasized their special doctrine and condemned those who did not come up to their belief. Baptists

---

1. Jones, "Sand and Sinning Saints," 8.

insisted upon "the baptism of believers by total immersion and the consequent denial of infant baptism."[2] The proponents of holiness emphasized that "all either go forward into holiness or backward into condemnation."[3] Pentecostals preached the need for speaking in tongues as evidence of the baptism of the Spirit. Evangelicals insisted upon the necessity of the new birth experience and the inerrancy of Scripture. It has always been the groups that boldly proclaimed their doctrine and defended their ideas publicly that have won converts to their beliefs and organizations. The true church should never be quiet but should defend its doctrines and practices.

No longer is the church on the offensive; it is on defense. No longer is it assumed the church has the truth. Atheists and agnostics have seized control of society's microphone. The church is considered scientifically, intellectually, socially, and politically backward and outdated. In society Christian ideas are no longer worth discussing. Christians are simply called intolerant bigots, and they are ignored. However, this has occurred as evidence regarding the accuracy of the Bible is becoming irrefutable. Yet, we are still losing the war. Scientific evidence proves a young earth, but evolution is winning. The value of a traditional two-parent family in society is overwhelmingly proven, but gay marriage and perverted sexuality have become accepted and legal. Science is clearly on the Christian side on every issue, but our response is rarely to attack back intellectually. Our reaction is to try to show we are nice people rather than boldly and intellectually defending our beliefs. The church is constantly on defense, and it is losing.

It is impossible to win a fight, either physically or intellectually, if a person is always on defense and never strikes back. In the last generation the church has lost the hearts and minds of America's people. All of this has occurred while trying to be nice and not offend others. This is a noble goal; but the opponents of Christianity meanwhile have been abusive, rude, cruel, and sometimes even riot; yet, they are winning the hearts of America. Non-Christians of today have proven that a constant, bold, uncompromising repetition of a belief always wins, even if it is a lie and its proponents are mean and hateful.

Increasingly, Christian beliefs and values have been marginalized. For a time only the elite opposed Christianity; but now in the news media, social media platforms, public schools, and major universities genuine Christians are viewed as a fringe group that is a threat to society. Josh McDowell said, "Society around you is undergoing what may be the fastest, most ominous cultural change in human history. . . . As a result, we may very well wake

---

2. McBeth, *Baptist Heritage*, 79.
3. Godbey, *Holiness or Hell*, 75.

up in the not-so-distant future in a culture that is not only unreceptive but openly hostile to the church and the gospel of Jesus Christ, a culture in which those who proclaim the gospel will be labeled as bigots and fanatics."[4] This prediction, published back in 1998, has become alarmingly true. Who would have believed a few years ago that Christians would be fired from their jobs or face criminal legal consequences for simply holding traditional family values?[5]

The church in Acts did face fierce persecution, in some instances even martyrdom, but society and legal authorities could not silence the message. Those disciples had the truth, they believed in that truth, and they refused to be silenced. The modern church is simply not following biblical methodology. Yes, many places do have billboards or other messages promoting Christianity, but rarely on battleground issues. If the church does take one of the key issues and fight back, it is often poorly done and not with an intellectual approach. One example is the Westboro Baptist Church, which protests all over the country and makes statements such as "God hates fags."[6] Neither Christ nor the early church made these kinds of wild, untrue, and emotional statements. People like this do far more harm than good. What is needed is a straightforward but uncompromising intellectual message that is constantly repeated in order to win in the battle of ideas. It is rare to change the mind of a person who is firmly opposed; it is usually unnoticed bystanders who are listening to or reading the arguments that are convinced. The war is won by constantly proving to those undecided bystanders the validity of our message.

One area in which the church has outspokenly defended its values is in its opposition to abortion. We are gaining some ground in convincing society it is wrong, although the opposition is just as loud and vehement as the church has been on the issue. A straightforward approach providing evidence that abortion is murder, and constantly attacking on the issue, has worked. The church was more concerned about saving a child's life than it was about not offending people. Sociologists have noted that in the battle for the hearts and minds of people, the stronger, more aggressive group wins.

This war is not only between society outside the church and those within. The greatest battle is occurring internally in the church. We are

---

4. McDowell and Hostetler, *New Tolerance*, 9.

5. There are a number of examples of intolerance of Christians which are occurring: such as a county clerk going to jail for refusing to give a marriage license to a gay couple; a baker who was fined for refusing to make a cake for a gay wedding; a court nominee who was aggressively challenged if she should be on the court because of her Catholic beliefs; along with many other instances.

6. This is the name they use for their website.

losing our own people. Many people may attend on Sunday who do not believe gay marriage is wrong or may believe in evolution. Furthermore, often a church person's lifestyle and attitudes are almost totally the same as the world at large. According to studies, Christians "think and behave no differently from anyone else."[7] Young people may be sitting in the pew but no longer accept the truth of the Bible. To many it is a book of fairy tales while the public school teaches science. In addition, young people have grown up in a culture that totally accepted any immoral practice. They do not see certain sinful practices as morally wrong but as merely an alternative lifestyle. The foundations must be rebuilt, beginning with winning our own people back to God's values. Boldly preaching the doctrine of the Bible on controversial issues is quite radical in many places and would cause much opposition. Some members would reject the change and leave the church; but without a return to Christian morality, the church itself has no long-term future. A church without God or his values, if it even survives, is not worth having; all it does is confuse others about what Christianity truly is.

The ultimate answer is we must have a moving of God. Revival which stirs people from their lethargy and lukewarmness is the only answer. We cannot change the hearts of people. Sin is too embedded in their minds and behavior, but God can do in an instant what we have failed to accomplish for years. It was the moving of God in the Great Awakenings which saved America from the perils of the Enlightenment. We must have another great awakening today!

Conservative evangelical, Pentecostal, Mennonite, and Holiness churches have spent the last fifty years failing to defend their reason for existence intellectually. These churches at one time lived a lifestyle that was far different from the culture around them, but most of them have now adopted the world's lifestyle. Others have not become worldly but often have seen little or no growth, and some denominations are collapsing. These denominations and churches should be growing according to many sociological studies, but they are not. Their problem is the failure to boldly defend their practices.

8. HARD WORK

Another biblical factor is the hard work and labor that are required in order for the task of evangelism to succeed. Jesus, in his ministry, was often up late at night working with the multitude and then up early to pray. Sometimes he and the disciples fled from the multitude because the work was so great

---

7. George Barna, https://ffrf.org/component/k2/item/18390-national-surveys-question-christian-morality.

(Mark 6:31). Paul stated that in his ministry at Thessalonica he "wrought with labour and travail night and day" (2 Thess 3:8). While this was referring to Paul's efforts to support himself as he evangelized, it does show his sacrificial endeavors. Paul admonished the Corinthian church to be "always abounding in the work of the Lord" (1 Cor 15:58). Others were commended for their efforts in sharing the gospel, such as the Ephesian church, which received this compliment from Christ: "I know thy works, and thy labour, and thy patience" (Rev 2:2).

As the people of our world have become more materialistically minded, life has become busier. Christians seem to have become less inclined to do the work of evangelization, as well as seemingly having less available time. A rising lethargy and unconcern for others has settled over the church. Any successful evangelism will take long, hard, consistent work, just as it did for Christ and the apostles. Anyone who gives of themselves to invest in the lives of others will be well rewarded by God. This is a difficult age, but minorities are being successfully evangelized.[8] Hispanics are perhaps the greatest source of growth in some groups. God has brought them to our communities. It is the church's responsibility to reach them with the gospel.

Yet, there are many places in which much effort has been put forth with few results. A person would expect that consistent evangelization efforts, such as a bus ministry which brings in numerous children from the community, would be constantly bearing fruit. Obviously, the attendance increases from the number of children who come, but often there are few long-term results. The children come and then drop out. Some parents attend for a while or even continue for a time on the fringes, but they never truly become established. It seems we must traverse sea and land to make one proselyte; however, Paul was able to take his methodology from one community to the next, establishing one church after another. The same is true of the Methodists, Baptists, and most evangelistic denominations of previous years.

God does reward his people for being faithful rather than being successful. The writer to the Hebrews said God "is not unrighteous to forget your work and labour of love" (Heb 6:10). Whether a person sees results or not, God is keeping track of our efforts. Eternity will reveal that those who sow the seed will share the reward of the harvest. Paul stated, "I have planted, Apollos watered; but God gave the increase. So then neither is he that planteth any thing, neither he that watereth; but God that giveth the increase" (1 Cor 3:6–7). We do want our efforts, though, to bring forth fruit for the kingdom of God.

---

8. Black, *Holiness Heritage*, 378–79.

We need examples of success which could then be copied and the pattern replicated across the country, but it seems what works in one place does not work elsewhere. The purpose-driven church concept has been tried repeatedly across our country, but the church is crumbling, not growing. Not only are most existing churches shrinking, but also every evangelical group is struggling to start new churches. In many groups more churches are closed than are opened. Those church plants which are successful are often simply transfers from another similar church. In most instances the number of people in overall attendance in a church or denomination are in decline.

CHAPTER 13

Defining Growth

Imagine a church which undergoes a great expansion in numbers. It goes from just a handful of attendees and then begins climbing into the hundreds or even thousands. New programs are started, and buildings are built and remodeled. Everything is positive it seems—but is it? Could these successful examples somehow be part of the cause of the crumbling of the American church? Some serious aspects must be analyzed. Where have the people come from? Is the church getting new converts? Are they saving their own children? Are new converts and their youth internalizing the beliefs and practices of the older generation? Is there a genuine transformation of the people from sinners and weak Christians into saints that model the character of Christ? Is genuine growth occurring in all aspects? Some of these churches may be like the Susquehanna River in central Pennsylvania. It is one of the widest rivers in the eastern United States, but in reality much of it is only waist deep. Is the American church becoming like that river, wide but with little depth? Are the churches full of more people, but ye like a river which instead of becoming deeper and carrying more water just becomes wider and shallower?

The concept of church growth needs to be divided into different types of growth. Numerical growth emphasizes numbers. Every person represents one soul, and it is very important that an increasing number of people be exposed to the truth of the gospel. An increase in numbers, however, may occur from people transferring from one good church to another. Another form of growth occurs when a church saves and keeps the young people raised in the church. Evangelistic or conversion growth occurs when unsaved, outside people are converted and brought into the church. Extension growth occurs when a church is involved in planting a new church. When a congregation or denomination reaches outside of its own ethnic group and is part of organizing another ethnic group into a congregation, this would be bridging growth.[1] Healthy denominations are effectively involved in all of these forms of growth. An organization which is not doing well is likely failing at several, if not all, of these categories of growth.

Growth is not limited just to numbers. Internal growth must be occurring among the people of the church. To have more people but less commitment from those which are in the church is not a good sign. Just like shrinking numbers, a decreased level of commitment will eventually spell the doom of the church. This problem is often acute among the second or third generation of people in the church or among newer converts. As the older generation dies off, the dedication needed to sustain the church also disappears.

TRANSFER GROWTH

Transfer growth is usually viewed positively by most churches. Any congregation should rejoice when an increasing number of people believe their spiritual needs are being met by that church. People want to attend where there is a warm, friendly group with which they can have fellowship. It is good to attend a place where there are activities in which one may become involved. Interesting and solid biblical preaching and teaching in a local congregation are attractive assets. Having buildings and facilities which are adequate and well-kept helps to encourage people to attend. People are looking for places where God is worshiped and the services are uplifting. Churches which exhibit these characteristics often have those who have transferred from other places.

People who move from church to church and are not loyal to any one place are rarely an asset, but it does say something positive about their feeling regarding where they are currently attending. Often transfer growth of this nature is not good for the receiving church. It may cause problems between the church from which they came and the new church. Those who jump from place to place will find that God will deal with their spiritual needs at the new place as well. They will then move on down the road to another church. While they are still attending, "church hoppers" have a tendency to complain and cause division. Usually people are a blessing to a church when they come, but tragically some people are more of a blessing when they go. From another perspective, though, "church hoppers" are

---

1. Hunter, *To Spread the Power*, 31–32. Some of the names for the differing types of growth were taken from this book.

needy people, and if their spiritual needs are met, they can become stalwart saints for God. Often good people can get stirred up by those who cause dissension but otherwise are not of the same critical nature. Sometimes the needs of those involved with the critical hypocrites are overlooked because the focus is on the outspoken nature of the critics.

The value system of our world measures success by means of numbers, but God measures success far differently. He is more concerned about transforming lives and preparing people for heaven. A pastor who is an excellent leader and has a pleasing personality often builds large churches, but it may be more personality driven rather than preparing more people for heaven. Sometimes transfer growth has occurred as people have moved from one area of the country to another. Among some groups the location of a Bible college in a specific area has become a magnet for cross-country transfers. Some of these transfers have been students who attended the college and stayed in the local area. In other instances, families have moved to raise their children in a better environment. Often the mainstays of a small local church have left, leaving a weakened local church behind. This is a positive statement about the area to which a person has moved and lends to the ease of building large churches, but it does not necessarily mean the kingdom of God has been increased. According to John Dickerson, "larger growing churches . . . continue to absorb folks from smaller churches. As a result, most of us have the perception that 'the church' is growing."[2] What is desperately needed is not transfer growth, but each local church gaining new converts from the local area.

BIOLOGICAL GROWTH

Biological growth occurs when children who are raised in a church which believes and practices the Bible choose to identify with its doctrines and practices and become a part of the group throughout their life. This is the story of one unfortunate church which has been repeated by many local churches and denominations across the country: The church had grown partly because its quality Christian day school was a magnet which drew people into the area. With the rise of home schooling and other Christian day schools, the number of those who moved into the area declined. Although the members were a good set of people with correct doctrine, they saw a high percentage of their young people simply choose not to become Christians. Others left the old-fashioned way for more worldly churches. This included some of the main leaders who were no longer young people. Attendance, which had

---

2. Dickerson, *Great Evangelical Recession*, 117.

peaked at over 150 in the 1970s, declined to only a third of what it had been. The major key to the decline of that local church was the failure to keep their own. If those people who grew up in that church and lived in the area still attended along with their families, that church would likely number several hundred.[3] At the same time that church, along with other similar churches in the area, began to lose the behavioral guidelines which had distinguished the church. The moderation of those standards did not result in keeping those who were pushing the boundaries; instead, the lack of a clear stand on issues led some to go to other churches, since the impression was given that the church's distinctives were unimportant.

This scenario has been repeated across the country. One area lost almost all of their young people between 1980 and 1995. This occurred while attempting to grow by downplaying the behavioral guidelines which had historically distinguished the group. Not only did the churches not grow, they also lost their conservative beliefs. Their future is not bright as the churches are predominantly filled with older people.[4]

> The majority of teenagers still attending church are already gone.
> —Ken Ham

Churches should naturally be growing just from the biological increase of families even without additional evangelism. Unfortunately, this is not the case; about 61 percent of young people drop out of church in their twenties.[5] Across America the church is failing to effectively convert the next generation. Young adults often leave the church due to reservations about the accuracy and the authority of the Bible.[6] Of those who left the church as young adults, more than 80 percent began having doubts about the Bible before graduating from high school. In this sense the majority of teenagers still attending church are already gone.[7] The failure to effectively convince young people of the academic validity of our theological worldview is the greatest reason why there is such a sharp loss of young adults in the church. After college graduation and marriage, "they have not returned to church, and many never will. Why not?

---

3. This is the story of the Church of God (Holiness) in Gravette, Arkansas. I am personally familiar with its story.

4. This happened to the Church of God (Holiness) churches in the Kansas City area. One young lady told me none of the young people she attended church with still attended one of the group's churches. Most of the young people had changed to Nazarene or Wesleyan Churches. This was also true of a number of older attendees.

5. Ham and Beemer, *Already Gone*, 25.

6. Ham and Beemer, *Already Gone*, 108.

7. Ham and Beemer, *Already Gone*, 32.

Because they don't believe in God or the Bible anymore."[8] Of those who leave, only 35 percent return to the church, while the others are gone permanently.[9]

EXTENSION AND BRIDGING GROWTH

Extension growth is planting new congregations. Many denominations have had a vision to establish a church of their organization in every community across the country. This was the vision that drove Francis Asbury. He wanted to establish congregations throughout every village in the early United States. Early in his ministry, when there were only a few preachers, he expressed, "I humbly hope before long about seven preachers of us will spread seven or eight hundred miles, and preach in as many places as we are able to attend."[10] Ultimately, "The seven preachers became a multitude and the seven or eight hundred miles grew into a continent."[11] Asbury's vision was caught by the other ministers of the movement, and its preachers all became home missionaries. "Every one of them was an extensionist enlarging his field of operations in every possible direction, opening a new preaching place at this point and that, his circuit in this manner growing steadily, until it had to be divided."[12] Galli and Olsen note, "When in October 1771, Asbury landed in Philadelphia, there were only 600 Methodists in America."[13] By the time of Asbury's death, "Methodism had grown under his leadership to 200,000 strong. His legacy continued with the 4,000 Methodists he had ordained: by the Civil War, American Methodists numbered 1.5 million."[14] Many other denominations or independent churches have followed the same pattern. Often a local church in a city would take responsibility to plant daughter churches in nearby towns or in other parts of the city. If America is ever won back to God it will be because godly people catch the vision of again reaching every person with the gospel message.

Bridging growth is the evangelization and establishment of the gospel among those outside of our culture. This would include foreign missions but also includes those from another country residing in America. One great opportunity for the church is the great number of those from around the world who have migrated to the United States. While world missions is still a great

---

8. Dickerson, *Great Evangelical Recession*, 100.
9. Dickerson, *Great Evangelical Recession*, 101.
10. Tipple, *Francis Asbury*, 118.
11. Tipple, *Francis Asbury*, 118.
12. Tipple, *Francis Asbury*, 120–21.
13. Galli and Olsen, *131 Christians Everyone Should Know*, 185.
14. Galli and Olsen, *131 Christians Everyone Should Know*, 185–86.

necessity, numbers of unevangelized people from other countries are just down the street or in the next neighborhood. Below is a chart which shows the rising number of immigrants and their percentage of the total population.[15]

Year	Size of Immigrant Population (Millions)	Immigrant Share of Total U.S. Population
1970	9.6	4.7
1980	14.1	6.2
1990	19.8	7.9
2000	31.1	11.1
2010	40.0	12.9
2016	43.7	13.5

This chart does not show the entire scope of the migration if their children are included. "Immigrants and their U.S.-born children now number approximately 86.4 million people, or 27 percent of the overall U.S. population."[16]

Many of these migrants to the United States, especially Hispanics, are open to the gospel; and many evangelical denominations have found an open door for evangelism. "Immigration, particularly from Mexico, has added steadily to the number of Latino Catholics. Meanwhile, conversion to other religions, particularly to evangelical Protestantism, has drawn down the number of Catholics. About one-in-ten Latinos was once a Catholic but is no longer holding that affiliation."[17] In addition, "the high number of self-identified charismatics among immigrants strongly suggests that Latin Americans entering the US . . . itself may be stimulating the shift to charismatic religion."[18]

SPIRITUAL GROWTH

Growth must not only occur in the number of people who attend a church but must also occur in the spiritual depth of the people who attend. One category of attendees is unconverted children from the community without any other church connection. Every effort must be taken to impact a person's life for God beginning when one is a child. Many churches have a children's ministry that is making an effort to reach this group, and some have been quite successful. Children often come for entertainment, fellowship, because their parents want them to, or even because they are bored.

---

15. Batalova et al., "Frequently Requested Statistics."
16. Zong et al, "Frequently Requested Statistics," para. 5.
17. Pew Research Center. "Changing Faiths," para. 15.
18. Hodges, "Immigrants Bringing Charismatic Flavor to U.S. Catholicism," para. 3.

This may take the form of Sunday school, bus ministry, or good news clubs. While this may greatly increase the total attendance, a person must remember these children are not yet the core constituency of the church. They are people who are being evangelized, and there is a hope that some will continue to identify with the church as they grow older. Yet, it is also true that only a small minority are successfully converted and become adult members and a core part of the church.

Unconverted adults may attend for many similar reasons as do children. They may enjoy the music, the programs, fellowship; or their attendance may simply be a traditional habit. As long as it is not compromising the gospel through its outreach methodology, a church should make every effort to encourage as many outside people to attend as often as possible. It gives the gospel a better chance of convicting them of their sin and changing their lives. These people, however, are not the core of the church; in time they will either get converted or drop out. The goal is to see their lives changed. In trying not to offend any attendees who are unsaved, a church must be careful not to compromise the gospel. While every effort must be made to be as kind and friendly as possible to those people, the church must also recognize it is necessary for a major transformation to occur at some point in an unconverted person's life if they are ever going to become a genuine, fervent Christian who is an upstanding church member.

Others who attend a church may have a measure of truth but not yet be completely part of the group. Some of these are unconverted people who believe this is the truth but have not yet committed their life to God. Others are new converts who do not yet truly realize the cost of serving God. Unconverted people at some point will have to decide their eternal destiny. The church must do everything in their power to continually encourage them toward serving God. Those who are newly converted will constantly face challenges in their lives as God deals with them concerning aspects of their lives which need to be brought under submission to God. Often they will face opposition from family members and friends who are opposed to anyone who decides to genuinely serve God. Challenges will come to these converts as God demands changes in lifestyle issues that are not Christian. They must choose whether to continue to serve God and give up those practices or whether to return to their formerly pagan culture. Some try to compromise by finding a church which will allow them to live as they wish and still claim to be saved; however, God is never satisfied with a half-hearted, compromising "Christian." God calls his people to present their entire bodies as a living sacrifice to God. It is impossible for a Christian to love both God and the world. Scripture says, "If any man love the world, the love of the Father is not in him" (1 John 2:15).

The final category is those who are converted, believe this is the truth, and are committed to this way. Every church should endeavor to bring all of its attendees to this goal. Allowing anyone to stop short is an incomplete success. Christ advocated in the Great Commission that a church should be "teaching them to observe all things whatsoever I have commanded you" (Matt 28:20). Jesus desired converts to believe and behave as he has commanded. A person must become a Christian not only in their heart but also in their head and in their lifestyle. The goal is to produce converts who have totally committed to continue with Christ at any cost. The life will then be marked by continual improvement as a person becomes more Christlike. These people will stand behind the church through difficulties, pay the bills, teach the classes, evangelize their neighbors, do all the work, and attend every service. The future of the church depends upon this committed minority.

This final deeply committed group is what is most lacking in the modern church world. The numbers in a movement may look good for Sunday morning attendance, but other services are about empty. The depth has disappeared. Far too many church members view church selfishly, asking, "What do I get?" Instead, a person should ask, "What does God want from me?" Lay participation and commitment is down, and churches often hire someone for the pastoral team to do what was done by laymen in the past. Instead of lay participation, even the church service has become a professional presentation. People attend sporadically whenever they wish rather than being personally committed to attending every service or activity. The paying of tithe and giving of special offerings is becoming a thing of the past, and personal commitment to soul-winning and evangelism is lacking. Attendees object if the church demands a change in their lifestyle, even defending blatant sin in some instances. Finally, if a church would demand a deeper spiritual commitment in their lives, attendees would simply change churches in order to find a more culturally accommodating church fellowship. Modern methodology which builds numbers without depth is destroying the church. Some places have built a large attendance but at the cost of future survival. The twenty-first-century church is now facing the consequences of cheap salvation. Christianity will either return to the true cost of the gospel or die numerically, financially, and, most importantly, spiritually.

IMPORTANCE OF QUALITY GROWTH

The policy of Christ was quality over quantity. He spent his ministry first focusing upon twelve disciples, even though he had a great number of other followers. Jesus preached to the multitudes in Galilee and at the temple and often emphasized the cost of the gospel. Due to this emphasis "many of his disciples went back, and walked no more with him" (John 6:66). Jesus demanded the rich young ruler pay the ultimate price of self-sacrifice in serving him. Christ knew his heart and demanded he give away his money, the main idol of his life. In the same way, Christ also demands we give up our most precious idol. For the church to follow Christ's example, the focus must be upon depth of spiritually rather than having many shallow believers.

A person must not make the mistake of assuming that becoming shallow will produce larger churches. Most denominations which compromise their beliefs for greater numbers do not see growth. If growth does occur in some localized areas (and it sometimes does happen), it will likely be in only a few churches, while most will begin a decline. In the long term, even those places which had growth will watch the succeeding generations of shallow Christians abandon Christianity.

In the business world, a superior product that focuses upon good quality will gain a good reputation, and its sales will continue to grow. Because of the higher cost for its quality, sales growth may not be spectacular; but the company will consistently keep growing as long as it has the best product on the market. Sometimes companies will use their reputation to sell an inferior product with their name. Spectacular growth and profits may follow for a short time but at a terrible cost. Their reputation disappears, which may eventually threaten the survival of the company. Poor-quality Christianity (if there is such a thing) has done the same thing with the gospel. It has brought in great numbers of half-hearted Christians but at the cost of the future of Christianity. No longer does the church have the power to transform lives, and the hypocrisy of the modern church has led to a negative cultural conception of Christianity.

Poor evangelistic methodology has the ability to erode the foundations of the church without successfully reaching people. The real issue is the number of new converts who personally know God and build the church long term. Poor methods may show growth for a time in numbers of attendees but will not expand the kingdom of heaven. If truth is deemphasized in order to reach more people, it will not only fail to change those people, but it will also encourage constituents to depart for a church with better programs. The final result of problematic evangelistic methodology for most local churches is smaller attendance and a loss of the doctrine and practices which once defined the church.

CHAPTER 14

The Answer for the Church

What can the church of today do to turn the situation around? It is obvious that new answers are needed. After fifty years of applying Church Growth movement and seeker-sensitive methodology, it is evident something has gone wrong. The church is now consumed with a desire to grow, but it is failing. Oh yes, there are multitudes of new megachurches, but overall most churches are in decline. The more emphasis many denominations have placed upon growth, the worse they have done. Not only has the church not grown, it has also lost the ability to set cultural guidelines. The Christian culture in America is gone, and the immorality of American society is setting the guidelines for the church. Almost no church leader in history would consider the current lifestyle of the church in America as morally acceptable. In many ways our day is similar to the day of Martin Luther when the church was consumed with immorality and materialism. In one sense our day is far worse. At least in the days of Luther the common person still believed in God and accepted Christianity as the truth. Atheism and agnosticism are currently overwhelming the Western world, and soon little truth may be left to revive.

The Western church is fatally sick. The church no longer has the power to evangelize and transform sinners, nor the power to keep our youth, or even the power for its members to live holy lives. Yet the church somehow staggers on; one year on life support follows another, but the final collapse is nearing. For many denominations, soon all that will be left of the once-vibrant body of believers in a town will be the tombstones—the monument of a beautiful building with a spire reaching to the sky. On its walls will be epitaphs telling about the vibrancy of the once-living organism; but soon the lights will go out, the last service will be conducted, and the last of the old saints will die. The doors will close forever, and the final witness to the truth in that place will be silenced. The tombstone remains, but only for a few more years until it is bulldozed. Then even its memory will be gone forever.

> While there is God there is always hope!

Yet, while there is life there is hope! While there is God there is always hope! Both biblical and scientific reasons explain the problem and give solutions to revive the church. Change is not easy, but the church will collapse both spiritually and numerically unless immediate steps are taken. God still wants to revive America and is waiting for us. A sinful world means even more broken people who need spiritual help. Some are still hungry for truth, and the church still has the only message of hope for our world. God will move, but it may be in judgment rather than in mercy. Yet, even in judgment his goal is an expression of his grace to bring America back to himself. A future hope lies in following the keys needed for the church.

NECESSITY OF REPENTANCE AND REVIVAL

In introducing theology for his first class in seminary, Dr. Henry Hollomon presented the question, "Can you have orthodoxy without orthopraxy, or can you have orthopraxy without orthodoxy? Or to say it another way, can a person have right beliefs without right practices, or right practices without right beliefs?"[1] This was a changing point in Bryan Loritts's life, and he accepted the premise that beliefs and behavior are intimately related. He concluded, "What I really believed was bound to ooze out through my behavior."[2] Psychologists would agree. Cognitive dissonance theory holds that people want their thoughts, beliefs, and attitudes to be in harmony with one another and with their behavior."[3] People will change either their behavior or their actions until their beliefs and behavior are in harmony. Sinful behavior will undermine correct theology.

A compromising Christianity will never survive. The church can only go forward by the power of God. It is not a human organization; it is a divine organism. God will not move in a church where sin is brazenly accepted. But is the modern church sinful? Francis Schaeffer stated in 1984, "We must

---

1. Loritts, "Life-Changing Question," 48.
2. Loritts, "Life-Changing Question," 48.
3. Bernstein and Nash, *Essentials of Psychology*, 550.

say with tears that, with exceptions, the evangelical church is worldly and not faithful to the living Christ."[4] The first of Martin Luther's 95 *Theses*, which began the Protestant Reformation, was: "All of a Christian's life is one of repentance."[5] After quoting Luther, Mark Driscoll then said, "That statement was not only the heart cry of the Protestant Reformation but was also the herald of every prophet God has ever sent."[6] J. I. Packer observed, "The essence of the gospel of Jesus Christ is repentance, and any theology that does not call people to repent is heresy."[7] Every spiritual awakening in history began with a call to repentance which specifically denounced the sins of the day and demanded the people of the church abandon their sins and give their lives to God. This is true of the Reformation, the Methodist revival, the Great Awakening, the Second Great Awakening, and has been a characteristic of revivals throughout history. The results of all of these revivals were the salvation of multitudes of souls, packed churches, and a changed culture.

Until people are willing to weep and cry over their godless behavior there is no hope. But when God's people "shall humble themselves, and pray, and seek my [God's] face, and turn from their wicked ways; [God says] then will I hear from heaven, and will forgive their sin, and will heal their land" (2 Chr 7:14). Without obedience God will not hear our prayers. Isaiah 59:2 says, "But your iniquities have separated between you and your God, and your sins have hid his face from you, that he will not hear." Yet the sinful church of today prays to a God who has closed his ears to their cry. People receive answers to their prayers "because we keep his commandments, and do those things that are pleasing in his sight" (1 John 3:22). No sinful church or person has any promise of ever receiving anything from God unless they are willing to repent. A sinful church is a powerless church. It may have an ability to gather people together for entertainment, excitement, or for an emotional high, but it does not have the power to transform lives. This is the major problem of today's church. We are trying every method possible to build the church in our own strength—over the top of our evil behavior. The biblical plan is for repentance to first occur. John the Baptist came preaching a message of repentance. Jesus' first message was repentance. The apostles at Pentecost demanded repentance, and Paul at Athens preached repentance to the gentiles. This message is in the forefront of the preaching in Scripture.

The people of the world are disgusted by the hypocrisy in the American church. When Christians live no different from the people who have

---

4. Schaeffer, *Great Evangelical Disaster*, 38.
5. Driscoll, *Call to Resurgence*, 182.
6. Driscoll, *Call to Resurgence*, 182.
7. Driscoll, *Call to Resurgence*, 182.

no profession, the unchurched have no confidence in their religion. When professing Christians tell the same filthy stories, use the same foul language, watch the same pornographic movies, excuse child sexual abuse, and participate in almost every evil of the world, it is no wonder that the unconverted are not attracted to the church. When sin does occur in the church, sometimes it is covered and hidden. If the news media uncovers the corruption, it is blasted across every news outlet; and once again the church's hypocrisy is exposed. This has made it difficult to attract and keep attendees in church. A study by Ken Ham and Britt Beemer reported, "Over half the people who have left the church are still solid believers in Jesus Christ. What they object to, however, is hypocrisy, legalism, and self-righteousness."[8] Francis Schaeffer said, "When the Scriptures are being destroyed . . . by cultural infiltration and compromise . . . we will cut the ground out from under the feet of our children, and we will destroy any hope of being the redeeming salt and light of our dying culture."[9] The world is not interested in a corrupt, evil collection of people who meet on Sunday morning. What does catch their attention, however, is when the power of God changes lives, and they see a body of believers for whom holiness of life has become the primary goal. In other words, the world is impressed by a religion whose followers' lives demonstrate evidence that they personally know God.

EVOLUTION AND THE INERRANCY OF THE BIBLE

The Bible is the foundation for everything in the Christian belief system. God's word was inerrantly given by him through the writers of Scripture. Anything that undermines the absolute trustworthiness of the Bible must be opposed at all costs. "The authority of the Scriptures is the foundation. If that is not protected, everything will eventually crumble. . . . We have to admit that the relevance of Scripture is already gone in this culture."[10] At the core of the issue is faith in God's creation of the world as described by God in Genesis. If the first three chapters of the Bible are not accepted just as they are written, then nothing else in Scripture can be considered authoritative. "As the church compromised on the issue of millions of years, subsequent generations were put on the slippery slide of unbelief."[11] Lee Strobel, who later became a Christian apologist, said, "I guess you could say I lost the last remnants of my faith in God during biology class in high school. So

---

8. Ham and Beemer, *Already Gone*, 118.
9. Schaeffer, *Great Evangelical Disaster*, 67.
10. Ham and Beemer, *Already Gone*, 90.
11. Ham and Beemer, *Already Gone*, 75.

profound was the experience that I could take you back to the very seat where I was sitting when I first was taught that evolution explained the origin and development of life."[12] There can be absolutely no compromise on this issue. Evolution is wrong, and the Bible is correct; but "our entire culture (including secular schools) is aggressively teaching the apologetics of evolution and secular humanism."[13] Either Christianity will prevail and destroy evolution or evolution will succeed and Christianity will be crushed. One or the other will be victorious. A Christianity that is soft on evolution will soon collapse and die. There can be no middle ground and there can be no compromise.

Tragically, the theory of evolution is sweeping through evangelical circles. The president of an evangelical college recently commented, "We are the only [regionally] accredited Christian college in the state that clearly teaches creation by God instead of evolution."[14] This is a very disturbing statement. He may have exaggerated the situation, but he believed that statement. To question the inerrancy of Scripture should never be a consideration for a Christian. It is no wonder evangelicals are in trouble; they are now following the same direction as other dying churches. Darwin's evolutionary concepts "are now, by and large, both welcomed and honored in the European church."[15] Evolutionary concepts were accepted by the American mainline churches early in the twentieth century. Now, the churches of Europe and mainline churches in America are dying; this is one of the major causes.

Evolution is also having an impact upon the evangelical movement. A study by the Pew Research Center in 2014 showed that 36 percent of evangelical Protestants accepted some form of evolution.[16] One major recent influence in undercutting Scripture is the BioLogos Foundation, founded by Francis Collins in 2007. Two of its core commitments are: "We embrace the historical Christian faith, upholding the authority and inspiration of the Bible. We affirm evolutionary creation, recognizing God as Creator of all life over billions of years."[17] The problem with these two statements is they are self-contradictory. It is impossible to accept the first three chapters of Genesis as inspired and authoritative and still believe in the theory of evolution. Nevertheless, BioLogos works to convince evangelicals that evolution and

12. Strobel, *Case for Faith*, 123.

13. Ham and Beemer, *Already Gone*, 49.

14. This incident occurred as my son was researching masters programs in 2018. Since there may be other colleges within that state that would disagree, I am not going to print the name of the state. The reality is that if the statement could be made, even if not technically correct, it shows serious problems within evangelicalism.

15. Ham and Beemer, *Already Gone*, 77.

16. See graph in Grossman, "Why Some Evangelicals Changed Their Minds."

17. https://biologos.org/about-us.

the Bible are not in conflict and can be harmonized. This foundation has held "several annual events in New York City, hosted by pastor Tim Keller, for leading pastors and theologians to gather with believing scientists for dialogue and worship."[18] Since its inception the foundation has grown to providing curriculum, workshops, a website, and many other materials to convince Christians of the validity of the theistic evolutionary position. While the goal of BioLogos may be to reconcile Christianity and science, the result is that numbers of evangelical Christians are abandoning the faith.

SCIENTIFIC PROBLEMS OF EVOLUTION

Not only is the Scripture clear that God did not use evolution to create the world, but also scientific evidence is now on the side of divine creation. Charles Darwin thought it was only a matter of time until missing evolutionary forms would be found; but over the last century, the evidence for evolution has faded. With the rise of DNA studies, it is evident that random evolutionary events could never have accidentally created life. Furthermore, random chance could never cause consistent positive changes in biological matter. Life is simply too complex. Scientists have been working for years in laboratories trying to create life, but have basically failed. If genuine life does not happen in a laboratory guided by the most brilliant scientists of our day, how could it have begun and then evolved into the variations of today? If life is ever created in a laboratory, it would prove one fact: it takes an intelligent being to create life. Considering the complexity of life on earth, it would take a being with infinite knowledge, namely God, to have developed life. One of the defenses used by creationists is the watchmaker theory. If a person discovers a watch in the forest, he assumes there is a watchmaker, although he has never seen or met the maker. The evidence is in the organized complexity. The same is true with this earth; its complexity proves the existence of a creator.

Another basic problem with evolution is the problem of beginnings. Something does not come from nothing. Either a person must believe in an eternal universe or an eternal God. One of the prevailing theories of beginnings is the big bang theory. Evolutionists think that at a point in time billions of years ago a tiny but almost infinite mass of energy exploded to form all of the matter and energy found in the universe. This one explosion randomly occurred just correctly to form matter, although the science of physics shows there was only an infinitesimal chance for this to occur. Within split seconds the universe was formed and stars and constellations

---

18. https://biologos.org/about-us.

had moved light years apart from each other. Although creationists disagree with evolutionists on when this event would have occurred, the big bang fits the account in Genesis 1:1. God spoke and the universe came into existence in a moment of time through an eternal, omnipotent, omniscient power.

Even the concept of trying to prove millions of years is in reality of no value for the evolutionists. We know God created in the first six days adult human beings along with mature and fruit-bearing trees. If God chose, he could have created a fully developed and mature earth that showed evidences of age. This is what God did with plants, animals, and people. Perhaps God placed the carbon fuels of coal, oil, and natural gas in the earth for man to later use. However, scientists who have studied the evidence can give dozens of scientific reasons which show that the beginning of this world occurred less than 10,000 years ago, exactly as taught in Scripture. Thankfully, scientists of our day who are Christians have begun to push back against the heresy of evolution. Organizations such as the Institute for Creation Research, Answers in Genesis, the Creation Museum outside Cincinnati, and the life-sized Ark Encounter in northern Kentucky are systematically proving the validity of the biblical creation account.

HORRIFIC IMPLICATIONS OF EVOLUTION

Any philosophical concept such as evolution has certain truths or implications which would logically follow. Evolutionist William Provine of Cornell University conceded that "if Darwinism is true, then there are five inescapable implications: there's no evidence for God; there's no life after death; there's no absolute foundation for right and wrong; there's no ultimate meaning for life; and people don't really have free will."[19] A few more concepts could be added to his list such as: the idea that man is not responsible to God; there is no sin or moral code; there is no need of a Savior; man is just another animal; racism and genocide are not wrong; and the earth should be worshiped as the provider of progress.

If God created man as described in the Bible then man is responsible to him as our Creator. Their disobedience in eating of the forbidden tree led them to be punished by God and laid the foundation for the existence of sin. Without the events described in these chapters it would be an impossibility for man to have a code of morality or to be accountable to God. Theistic evolution, which contains the concept that God used evolution to create the world, totally fails to establish man's accountability. It is impossible for man to evolve and to have the act of Adam and Eve which brought sin to the

---

19. Strobel, *Case for Faith*, 125.

world. If there is no sin, there is no need for a Savior; thus there would be no purpose for the existence of Christ since there is no sin from which to be saved. Evolution also destroys meaning and purpose in life, since without God, death is the end of life, and there can be no ultimate purpose. Radical environmentalists have tried to find meaning in the worship of the earth, since it seems man is created to worship; but why should a person worry about saving the earth if there is no true meaning to life? Would the earth and life really matter? What is the foundation for those moral beliefs?

Another major ethical problem is that racism and genocide are based upon Darwin's theory of evolution. Anyone who believes in the theory of evolution is philosophically a racist. This does not mean that a person understands or behaves according to his philosophy, but ultimately a culture moves in the direction of its philosophical foundation. The acceptance of evolution does mean Western culture, over time, will begin the extermination of the disabled, the objectionable, criminals, and those who are believed to be racially inferior humans. The mechanics of evolution is in variation within a species. The strong survive and pass along their traits through survival of the fittest. Evolution, accordingly, must accept that there would be variations within the human species. Namely, some humans would be superior to other humans in such aspects as intellect, strength, or other characteristics needed for survival; therefore, some people are racially better than other people. Therefore, our resources should be given to support the superior humans; and inferior people should be relegated to subhuman status. This is a horrific conclusion, but it is the only logical conclusion for Darwinian evolution. "Darwinism . . . promoted racism, justified social and political inequality, and glorified war. It also inspired Adolf Hitler and his ardent supporters to launch a world war and exterminate the Jews of Europe."[20]

Christianity teaches a far different philosophy. Scripture says, "And [God] hath made of one blood all nations of men" (Acts 17:26). Accordingly, all people are of equal value as descendants of Adam and Eve and equally loved by Christ. As followers of Jesus, Christians have always led the way in personally giving of themselves to care for the poor and needy, both in America and around the world.

To successfully evangelize, the church must emphasize once again the very foundation of creation by God and our personal accountability to him. The battle for our culture is first and foremost an intellectual battle. If a person does not believe in God, he will be almost impossible to reach for Christ. They may respect Christians, think highly of Christians, and appreciate the love Christians manifest to them, but ultimately it takes a belief in

---

20. McMillan, "Hitler, Darwin and the Holocaust," para. 5.

Christ to be saved. How can they believe in Christ when they do not believe in God? Furthermore, "Faith that is not founded on fact will ultimately falter in the storm of secularism."[21]

In the evangelization of young people and college students, the doctrine of creation should be one of the most effective tools. If young people are convinced of the validity of creation and the Scripture, they should come naturally to Christ. In addition, most people have never come to understand the horrific implications of evolution. They oppose racism, yet accept the very philosophy upon which racism is based. The contradiction between their beliefs and their foundational philosophy should be emphasized in evangelism. Pointing out the truth regarding the tie between evolution and racism should give them a desire to replace their unworkable philosophy with a solid intellectual system based upon Christianity.

A weakening of the authority of the Bible is another battle faced in our day. I remember the time that Nancy, a lady who attended my church, was not in church services. She was a new person but had been coming regularly. Her son had also begun attending a local Christian school connected with our organization. While visiting with her, I was informed her son had come home from school and told her she was going to hell because of a certain behavior of hers. While our church clearly believed this needed to change in her life, we certainly had not stated it that way, and neither had the teachers in the school. I carefully explained to her our biblical belief and how it related to Scripture, but I question that she even listened. Her response was, "I do not believe like you, and need to find a church which agrees with me." I tried to explain that the key was discovering the teaching of Scripture, not finding someone who agreed with her position. Unfortunately, she never returned. Sadly, her attitude is the common thought in America today. Our personal opinion and what we want to do is of more importance to us than God's word.

The church is no longer viewing Scripture as the source for the answers of life, and others use verses out of context to defend unbiblical beliefs. Deep biblical study, which at one time was common for laymen, is becoming rare. Sunday schools are dying because there is little interest in biblical study. What is left of Sunday school is for children and has become entertainment-driven rather than academic. Often theologians are more interested in applying modern philosophy rather than correctly interpreting Scripture. Most of the theological disagreements today would end if the Bible were taken literally for what it taught. If counseling disagrees with Scripture, modern counseling is followed. If modern concepts of discipline contradict Scripture, then the church follows the new ideas. If what a person wants to do is forbidden by

---

21. Ham and Beemer, *Already Gone*, 49.

Scripture, then a person simply finds a church that agrees with them. Evangelicals must return to the historic concept of simply accepting God's word for what it says, believing it, and then following it.

> Most theological disagreements would end if the Bible were taken literally for what it taught.

RESTORING THE DOCTRINE OF THE PERSEVERANCE OF THE SAINTS

The focus of this book is not to debate theology but to analyze what has changed to discover the causes of the loss of growth. When the Southern Baptist denomination has a history of constant rapid growth, as well as creating a Christian culture, for 250 years, and then falters, it should be asked: What changed? One major change was from the traditional Calvinist position to a modified Calvinist position. Modified or Neo-Calvinists have changed the concept that a saint perseveres to the end to the idea that God preserves a person in their salvation. Many eternal security proponents openly state that no matter what a person does, he or she is still a child of God and will go to heaven. This differs from the traditional Calvinistic belief which taught that if God converted an individual that person persevered in righteousness till the end of life. John Calvin wrote, "Those who fall away have never been thoroughly imbued with the knowledge of Christ but only had a slight and passing taste of it."[22] Falling away was considered evidence the individual had never been saved. Calvin also believed those who fell away perished: "In the elect alone he implants the living root of faith, so that they persevere even to the end. Thus we dispose of the objection, that if God truly displays his grace, it must endure forever. There is nothing inconsistent in this with the fact of his enlightening some with a present sense of grace, which afterward proves evanescent."[23]

The concept that a person can live a life of willful sin in defiance of righteousness and still go to heaven is a recent change of doctrine. The belief of the Baptists on the frontier in 1798 is shown in a church constitution which states, "We believe that the saints shall persevere and never finally fall away."[24] In 1913, the Sunday School Board of the Southern Baptist Conven-

---

22. Torrance et al., *John 11–21 and 1 John*, 258.
23. Calvin, *Institutes*, 3.2.11.362.
24. McBeth, *Baptist Heritage*, 225.

tion published a book, *What Baptists Believe,* which defined Baptist beliefs. In the section on "Perseverance of the Saints" it states, "We believe that such only are real believers as endure unto the end; that their persevering attachment to Christ is the grand mark which distinguishes them from superficial professors."[25] In another place this book states,

> A man may be self-deceived. He may have refused the complete surrender of his heart which the gospel demanded, believing that he could obtain eternal life at smaller cost. He may have persuaded himself that he has indeed obtained life. In that hope he may have entered into the discharge of the duties of the Christian life, and long have met no test which he did not appear to sustain with fair credit. Self-deceived, he has been lulled into a false security. The awakening comes with some unexpected test, some temptation for which he was not prepared. Then it is revealed that the life of the past was an outer conformity and not the result of an inner change. As long as life lasts there is the possibility of such failure. If it comes even at the last of life, it is as sure proof as it had come earlier that the soul has not passed from death unto life.[26]

Southern Baptists, as well as other evangelicals, have changed to a great degree on this doctrine. Yet, David Buschart, in his recent book, *Exploring Protestant Traditions,* gave the historic position from their doctrinal statements as though it were still accurate today. He described Baptists as believing that

> those who are regenerate will manifest this reality by believing the truth, trusting Jesus Christ for salvation from sin, giving verbal testimony to this, and living a life of obedience to God's directives set forth in the Bible. Thus, sanctification is the evidence of regeneration . . . and those who have experienced regeneration will manifest this in a sanctified life.[27]

Most pastors today would agree that Bushart is describing the ideal while this is not the common life of very many evangelicals at present; however, this concept of holy living is what all evangelical Christianity believed and practiced at one time. When this was true, the church was rapidly growing; but by excusing willful sin, the church has lost its ability to grow. If the church is not different from the world, non-Christians view

---

25. Wallace, *What Baptists Believe,* 118.
26. Wallace, *What Baptists Believe,* 121–22.
27. *New Hampshire Confession,* "Articles 7 and 10," quoted by Bushart, *Exploring Protestant Traditions,* 167.

it as hypocritical and as having nothing to offer. To effectively address the problem, the church must identify what concepts are hindering evangelism, even if it does not align with one's doctrine. This change in theological beliefs is one of the keys as to why the church is losing its own children and failing to effectively evangelize.

NECESSITY OF THE LORD'S DAY

Another major change in society and in the church is the observance of the Lord's Day as a time set apart for rest and worship of God. Most evangelicals in the last two generations have come to the conclusion that the concept of the Sabbath day is an Old Testament belief that was not required for the New Testament church; but almost every religious group before 1950 dogmatically insisted upon keeping the Lord's Day. It was even encoded into law in most of the states. For example, in the 1980s, Arkansas did not allow most businesses to be open on Sunday.[28] Baptists dominated the religious scene in that state, and it was their influence that had created those laws in Arkansas as other Christians had done in most other states.

It makes simple logical sense that when a religious group sets apart a day in which to worship God, the people will meet together in church for that purpose. When Sabbath-keeping is no longer considered a necessity, many of the people will get jobs on that day, use it as a day for vacation, or simply do tasks around the house. In previous times these activities would have been forbidden or strongly discouraged. Previously, the church had not competed with every possible activity on Sunday; instead, the people set this day apart as a time for God. When the concept of setting apart Sunday for God is undermined, along with the belief that it is not necessary for Christians to attend church, it is a wonder that as many people as do show up in church. Nevertheless, habit is a strong force, and most older people will continue to practice the behaviors in which they have been reared; however, evidence shows the younger generation is less committed, their attendance has become more irregular, and many professing Christians rarely come to church unless it is convenient. A philosophical change of belief, such as setting the Lord's Day apart, usually becomes more evident in the second generation.

---

28. My job at that time was at a Walmart store. The store was forbidden by state law to be open. I remember the law changed sometime after 1982, when I no longer worked there.

UNDERMINING THE BORN-AGAIN EXPERIENCE

Another problem is the eternal security doctrine has been mixed with a weakened Arminian theology in the issue of lordship salvation. Opponents say it is a "false doctrine that says that in order for a person to be saved he must make Jesus the Lord of his life."[29] They oppose requiring repentance from sin as a necessity for salvation, saying, "We have to repent only of the thing that makes us unsaved, and that is unbelief."[30] Those who do not believe in lordship salvation teach that a person can accept Christ's salvation while rejecting Christ as Lord of their life. They teach that a person should live a good life but may continue in willful sin, but now since they have been saved he or she can never be lost. All that remains of this Christianity is a fragmented combination of Calvinism and a cheapened Arminian theology, which allows for a watered-down born-again experience added to an eternal security belief that allows for deliberate sin in the life of a Christian. This deadly doctrinal twist is permeating the Christian world of today. If it continues, it will undermine and destroy Christianity and the Christian church. Millions of people are relying upon this false doctrine for their salvation, but in reality they are lost. Accordingly, this is one of the most dangerous false beliefs of our day. Most of those who follow this doctrine are lost and need to be saved.

---

29. Hyles, *Enemies of Soul Winning*, 1.
30. Hyles, *Enemies of Soul Winning*, 31.

CHAPTER 15

The Answer for the Holiness Movement

The Holiness movement seems to be following the pattern set by the Methodist Church. When the Holiness people left, the Methodist Church lost its rapid growth rate.[1] At first, membership numbers continued to increase, but at a slower rate; then in the 1960s, total membership began to decline; and in the last fifty years the membership of the United Methodist Church has dropped 33 percent.[2] It has declined from a membership of 11,026,976 to 7,391,911.[3] This trend is evident in other mainline churches as well. The Holiness movement is following the same course set by the Methodist Church. Explosive growth characterized the Holiness movement when the group was emphatic about its doctrine and strict in its enforcement. In the 1950s and 1960s, the emphasis upon a distinctive lifestyle declined and many conservatives left. Then, just as occurred among the Methodists of an earlier time, the larger Holiness denominations continued to grow, but at a slower rate. A change in theology to a relational model of holiness began in the 1970s, which weakened the radicalism of those Holiness churches. Along with the change in lifestyle and Holiness theology, many of the educational leaders of the movement in the last few decades stopped accepting the traditional belief in the inerrancy of the Bible. As each of these developments occurred, it was followed by a decline in growth rates. Currently, growth rates are flat, both in numbers of congregations and in membership, with most denominations showing a slight decline.[4]

1. Finke and Stark, *Churching of America, 1776–1990*, 145–47.
2. Finke and Stark, *Churching of America, 1776–1990*, 248–49.
3. hirr.hartsem.edu/research/fastfacts/fast_facts.html.
4. hirr.hartsem.edu/research/fastfacts/fast_facts.html.

IDENTIFYING THE PROBLEM

When any organization is doing phenomenally well and then it begins to decline, it should lead to serious introspection. Something has obviously changed. But what? Is the problem within the denomination? Does the difficulty lie in societal changes? Are similar organizations likewise experiencing trouble? Is the problem primarily a marketing issue, or are there fundamental adjustments which must be made? Finally, are there examples of groups which are successful? The answer is complex. Every one of the above questions should be analyzed to determine corrections which should be made. This study gives preliminary answers to these questions; however, much further study should be done to work toward practical solutions to the dilemma.

The Holiness movement has historically based its outreach upon the aggressive preaching of holiness, both in doctrine and lifestyle, as the means to successfully build a church. A philosophical change occurred at mid-century concerning presuppositions about church growth. Many Holiness people came to believe the most effective way to reach people was to downplay the differences in lifestyle standards in order to not offend people. Yet, that common assumption is not correct. When a church is strict and fervently believes in its cause, it grows. "The burgeoning churches, almost by definition tend to have good leaders with a more orthodox theology. They have energy. They make demands on people. Many growing churches are like the Marine Corps: The harder you make it, the more people love it and want to be a part of it."[5] A soft, mushy, nondemanding Holiness movement just doesn't cut it. The cost to be holy has always been high, and this will never change.

This debate between strictness and growth had been faced by the founders of the Holiness movement a century earlier. Holiness leaders John Wesley Redfield and Benjamin T. Roberts both experienced the same growth philosophy a century earlier. Redfield emphasized that the Holiness message was the way to keep converts from jumping to more worldly churches.[6] Roberts blasted the "worldly" Methodists of his day for substituting "parties of pleasure, oyster suppers, fairs, grab bags, festivals, and lotteries" rather than choosing to "rely for the spread of the gospel upon the agency of the Holy Ghost, and the purity of the church."[7] In 1853, he blamed the low level of spirituality, the lack of enforcement of the discipline, and a tide of

---

5. Olasky, "Creative Philanthropy," 29.
6. Terrill, *Life of Rev. John Wesley Redfield, M. D.*, 117.
7. Zahniser, *Earnest Christian*, 89–90.

worldliness for the numerical decline of the Genesee Conference.[8] This would have been one of the few Methodist Conferences that was not experiencing rapid growth. A generation later, both W. B. Godbey and John T. Hatfield struggled with the same issue in the Methodist Church. In one of Godbey's circuits, the members who opposed his uncompromising standards hauled Godbey before the presiding elder and stated, "You will have to take this man away from us. He will smash everything and we'll never pay half of our assessments."[9] Godbey was exchanged to a neighboring conference. In that place, Godbey had 400 conversions; but the circuit he left "tinkered along all the year with corn-stalk fiddles and never had a soul converted."[10] Hatfield mentions that a group of elders once barred him and other evangelists from holding meetings on their charges. Another elder, however, supported Hatfield and provided him with places in which to labor. In that one district, Hatfield reported more than 3,500 conversions that year while preaching the radical holiness message. That district had far more conversions than the other five combined.[11]

By the mid-twentieth century, however, many Holiness people felt the emphasis upon the conservative lifestyle hindered growth. One Wesleyan Methodist leader felt the choice was between evangelism and legalism and was "reluctant to require anything 'nonessential' of converts lest artificial barriers keep them out of the kingdom and out of the church."[12] A Nazarene general superintendent stated in the *Herald of Holiness* that he feared when too much concern was given to external standards it would lead to "a maze of darkness and chaos" and cause many souls to be lost forever.[13] Neither the leaders nor most of the people in the Nazarene and Wesleyan Churches were planning to abandon the historic beliefs and practices of their denominations; however, they were willing to deemphasize some of the standards they considered "nonessential," hoping to obtain growth. They were wrong; instead of success in expanding the church, the following decades saw a massive decline in growth rates.

Evangelism before 1970 "generally meant getting people converted the old-fashioned way by holding revivals, sponsoring camp meetings, and giving altar calls in church services."[14] These methods were soon replaced

8. Zahniser, *Earnest Christian*, 59.
9. Godbey, *Holiness or Hell*, 19.
10. Godbey, *Holiness or Hell*, 19.
11. Hatfield, *Thirty-Three Years a Live Wire*, 93.
12. Haines and Thomas, *Outline History of the Wesleyan Church*, 117.
13. Purkiser, *Called Unto Holiness*, 2:31.
14. Black and Drury, *Story of the Wesleyan Church*, 230.

by concepts such as Bill Bright's "The Four Spiritual Laws," or *Evangelism Explosion* used by D. James Kennedy.[15] John Maxwell was brought into the Wesleyan Church and helped to make personal evangelism a dominant theme for Wesleyans.[16] During the 1980s, evangelism efforts also brought a renewed focus upon church attendance. Seeker-sensitive ideas from Bill Hybels channeled through John Maxwell became the mantra for how to build a church.[17] The Holiness movement began using the same seeker-sensitive model as other evangelical churches. Some churches were successful, and the Holiness movement entered into the megachurch scene. The Wesleyan Church is a good example; by 2010, almost one-quarter of all Wesleyans were attending the twenty-five largest churches.[18]

Dynamic leadership, well-run programs, and financial ability have enabled megachurches to succeed in a broader evangelical context, but underlying their successes are serious problems. Most of the denomination is not seeing the benefits. About the turn of the century into the new millennium, the Church of the Nazarene, the Wesleyan Church, the Free Methodist Church, and the Church of God (Anderson, Indiana) all began to slide toward stagnation. Yet, during this period of decline in growth, there was a rising focus upon evangelism and attendance. Something is seriously wrong when increased efforts and focus do not lead to overall positive results. The problem is the growth philosophy. It is impossible to merge the popularity-driven growth ideology of today with the Holiness message which demands a radical consecration of one's life to God.

THE HOLINESS MOVEMENT AND HISTORICAL GROWTH

The Methodist Church and the followers of Wesley have had more of God's power in transforming the world than almost any other movement in world history since the days of the early church. It had an impact upon both of the Great Awakenings in America. Its emphasis upon experiential religion helped to revive the belief in a born-again conversion experience; and Methodism influenced the beginnings of Protestant missions.[19] Within 40 years after its arrival in America, the Methodist Church had become the largest denomination in the United States. Its growth continued throughout the nineteenth century; however, around 1900, two events changed the

---

15. Black and Drury, *Story of the Wesleyan Church*, 230–31.
16. Black and Drury, *The Story: The Wesleyan Church*, 234.
17. Black and Drury, *The Story: The Wesleyan Church*, 248.
18. Black and Drury, *The Story: The Wesleyan Church*, 250.
19. Andros, *Wesley's World Parish*, 33, 52.

trajectory of Methodist Church growth: the most outspoken Holiness proponents left the group and theological liberalism overtook the theology in denominational colleges. Several decades of slow rates of increase followed, and then the denomination began shrinking in the 1960s.

Both the Holiness movement and the Pentecostal groups have a background in Methodism. Wesley believed a person could live a life without committing willful sin. He also advocated a second experience of grace which purified a person from the sin nature and baptized a person with the Holy Spirit. The greatest time of success for holiness people was in the late 1800s. Their doctrine was influencing many people in other circles. Charles Finney the Congregationalist, A. B. Simpson and R. A. Torrey, both Presbyterians, and Dwight L. Moody, the independent evangelist, along with many others, accepted the Holiness message.[20] The Salvation Army, which had arrived from England, also promoted this belief. However, Methodist Church leadership in the late 1800s began to abandon the doctrine of holiness and applied pressure on many Holiness proponents to leave the denomination. These people, as they left the Methodist Church, organized their own denominations or associated with other similar people who had previously left the Methodist Church. A division over whether speaking in tongues was the evidence of the baptism of the Holy Spirit caused the Holiness movement and the Pentecostal churches to go differing directions.

Many of the Holiness people gathered together in the Church of the Nazarene or the Pilgrim Holiness Church, which later became part of the Wesleyan Church. The Nazarenes, at their fiftieth anniversary in 1958, had a denomination with more than 4,000 churches and almost 300,000 members in the United States. Its rapid growth slowed after that point, but by its 100th anniversary there were over 5,000 churches and over 600,000 members.[21] Nazarene membership in the US has now has begun to shrink. What has changed to cause this to happen?

For any group to grow it must effectively articulate and propagate its purpose for existence. According to the official history of the Church of the Nazarene, the group "saw its reason for being in the special advocacy of holiness of heart and life."[22] At the end of fifty years, in 1958, the author of their official history stated, "There is no indication . . . of any real change of direction or purpose in the church. If anything, there seems to have been an even greater consciousness of the importance of holding to that course. The church . . . was still very much a holiness church and still very

20. Black, *Holiness Heritage*, 39, 45, 163.
21. http://www.thearda.com/Denoms/D_1441.asp.
22. Purkiser, *Called Unto Holiness*, 2:10.

much concerned with taking the whole gospel to the whole world."²³ When that denomination, along with other Holiness people, was exploding with evangelistic power, they thoroughly believed in their doctrine and lived their holiness theology out in their lives. When the Holiness movement was strict, emphasized and defended their doctrine, and expected their people to live accordingly, the denomination grew.

Since the 1960s, Holiness people, including Nazarenes, have been deemphasizing and weakening their beliefs. Traditional holiness theology taught two instantaneous works of grace: a new birth experience which justified a person from committed acts of sin, and a second experience of grace that purified the heart from the sin nature. However, a new model for the holiness doctrine was developed which could be described as "a major paradigm shift in the Holiness movement to a relational way of thinking about sin and holiness."²⁴ The relational holiness doctrine developed by Mildred Wynkoop saw holiness as a dynamic relational process instead of two objective works of grace as traditionally believed.²⁵ Wynkoop's relational model not only "called into question the relevance of the traditional understanding of the doctrine of entire sanctification,"²⁶ but also the Wesleyan understanding of the definition of sin. She understood sin as "love gone astray" and "the distortion of love" rather than as traditionally believed by the denomination as a "voluntary violation of a known law of God."²⁷

The new concept of relational holiness took root in the Church of the Nazarene and "at the end of the 20th century, there was no substantial agreement in the denomination over what it meant to be 'entirely sanctified.' The Church of the Nazarene no longer had a precisely articulated definition of their distinctive doctrine, the doctrine that at one time had been their sole reason for being."²⁸ Holiness people were accepting a different theology from what they believed in the days of denominational growth. According to Richard S. Taylor, one of their leading theologians, this was "a major contributing cause of the staggering of the holiness ranks."²⁹ Keith Drury, a Wesleyan scholar, stated, "Gradually the theology among our [holiness] people became the same generic evangelical soup served at any

---

23. Purkiser, *Called Unto Holiness*, 2:10.
24. Tredoux, *Mildred Bangs Wynkoop*, 15.
25. Tredoux, *Mildred Bangs Wynkoop*, 4.
26. Quanstrom, *Century of Holiness Theology*, 141.
27. Quanstrom, *Century of Holiness Theology*, 144, 190, quoting *Church of the Nazarene Manual*.
28. Quanstrom, *Century of Holiness Theology*, 174.
29. Drury et al., *Counterpoint*, 50.

other evangelical church. Holiness people became evangelical people,"[30] and today have merged into the evangelical mainstream.

> A Church can sell its message only as long as its people are fervently convinced of its validity.

Sociological studies explain the difficulties in outreach which the Holiness movement is currently undergoing. Religious groups which grow are those who are dogmatic, strict, and absolutist about their beliefs. In contrast, the Holiness movement for the last several decades has emphasized having a good image; dealing gently with people, especially sinners and new converts; working cooperatively with other groups who are not of our beliefs; and opposing those who are dogmatic or considered legalistic. In previous generations when the Holiness movement was growing rapidly, Holiness people believed in the necessity of holiness and expected their people to live according to biblical guidelines. Currently, even Holiness people have become silent about the experience of holiness, and little is said about the Holiness message outside the doors of the church. Keith Drury stated that one of the reasons the movement died was "we quit making holiness the main issue."[31] Although Drury was addressing Holiness theology rather than growth, it is also true this loss of fervency for the Holiness message is a major factor in the decreasing growth rate of the Holiness movement.

Successful salesmen are always thoroughly convinced of the need for their product and certain of its abilities. A church can sell its message to others only when the people of the church are convinced of the necessity of their beliefs and practices and are willing to defend them. Yet, for much of the last fifty years, Holiness people have avoided defending their doctrine in the public arena. The theology of the Holiness movement demands more of its people than the religion promoted by many others, and for this reason Holiness churches should be seeing growth. Wesleyan theology demands a transformation of life, but this conflicts with the seeker-sensitive model for building a megachurch. Holiness churches have been confronted with a dilemma. They must either abandon their theology or the popular model of growth. They choose to accept the popular concept; accordingly, the doctrine of holiness has become a "dead" doctrine, and the concept of "transformational conversion" is quickly disappearing.[32] In accordance with its growth model, the Holiness movement has simply become another

---

30. Drury et al., *Counterpoint*, 20.
31. Drury et al., *Counterpoint*, 20.
32. Drury et al., *Counterpoint*, 24.

evangelical church, unwilling to clash with the religious culture regarding its distinctive beliefs. By compromising on its very reason for existence, it is no wonder the movement has lost its ability to sell its beliefs in our world.

This false concept, that the lowering of demands promotes successful evangelism, has led not only to the loss of a biblical lifestyle in the larger holiness denominations, but also to the decline of growth. Denominations which are socially strong will "tend to increase in membership and weak ones to diminish . . . [and] strong organizations are strict.[33] According to Dean Kelley, this strictness is the major factor in building a strong organization. Roger Finke and Rodney Starke researched the same concept in their historical study of American church growth. They said, "When the cost of membership increases, then net gains of membership increase also."[34]

At one time, differences in theology and behavior were emphasized by Holiness people as the means of outreach. Now, even among conservatives, these differences have been minimized in the process of evangelization. The Holiness movement has moved from evangelism based upon the emphasis of truth to the use of fellowship and entertainment as the means of outreach. In many places, the Holiness movement is using the same message and methods as other evangelical churches. Yet, the theology of the Holiness movement demands more of its people; and a weak, unassuming religion does not fit their background.

THE ANSWER FOR THE CONSERVATIVE HOLINESS MOVEMENT

All holiness people have not abandoned the conservative lifestyle or the doctrines of their heritage; however, the Conservative Holiness Movement (CHM) has also failed to grow, and losses have now reached a crisis point. Unless things change, this movement will shrink to almost nothing within a few decades. Michael Avery, the former president of God's Bible School, called this the "elephant in the room that nobody wants to talk about!"[35] He said, "The movement is in a state of serious decline. It has failed to grow numerically by means of new conversions, while membership rolls in some of the largest and oldest denominations have decreased as much as 60 percent."[36] Almost all of the denominations in the CHM have declined in numbers of churches over the last two decades, and the overall average

---

33. Kelley, *Why Conservative Churches Are Growing*, 95.
34. Finke and Stark, *Churching of America, 1776–1990*, 255.
35. Avery and Smith, *Call*, 164.
36. Avery and Smith, *Call*, 164.

church attendance is down. The people in the Conservative Holiness Movement are very dedicated, yet their efforts often only result in a marginal number of conversions which continue to attend church.

Conservative Holiness churches predominantly arose from the Holiness movement in the 1950s and 1960s over standards regarding holy behavior; however, they failed to adequately defend their differences in the marketplace of ideas. Their message rarely reached beyond the four walls of their own churches. Often, the group deemphasized their guidelines in order for their churches to better evangelize and grow, but this has not worked; instead, their own people have lost their belief in the standards, and, as a result, many left conservative churches for, and adopted, a less strict lifestyle. This has made it difficult to win converts to a church that no longer believes in its reason for existence.

While biblical accuracy and behavior based upon absolute truth should be the foundation of growth for any church, unfortunately it is not the doctrinal orthodoxy of the message that causes a group to grow. Religious organizations have promoted some of the strangest and most indefensible beliefs; yet if they fervently believed their message and aggressively promoted it, these groups grew rapidly. Certain sociological characteristics lead to numerical growth even among cult-like organizations. In contrast, conservative Holiness people are only trying to conserve the beliefs and practices which have always been characteristic of holiness people as well as many other evangelicals. If any strict group should be able to adequately promote and sell their doctrine and practices to others it should be the conservatives; however, the group overall retreated into its own shell and had little to do with other churches, or when involved with others failed to strongly defend their beliefs.

If the CHM revives (and in many places it needs a resurrection), it will be through a fervent, uncompromising advocacy of their ideals in the public theological marketplace. It is an absolute necessity for any strict group to constantly defend both among themselves and to outsiders the reason for their existence in order to grow or to even keep their own from leaving. Holiness people are theologically distinctive in two basic theological beliefs which must be strongly emphasized. These are:

- All people who are Christians live without sinning as sin is defined by the Wesleyan-Arminian movement.
- God has a second definite work of grace in which the heart is purified from inbred sin, and the person at the same time is filled with the Holy Spirit.

Conservative Holiness people have followed the beliefs of John Wesley that Christians do not willfully disobey God. If a person deliberately disobeys God, it is necessary to go to God and ask for forgiveness. He will readily forgive and restore. Failure to obey God will cause the loss of one's salvation. Wesleyans believe the sin principle of the heart may be destroyed and the heart purified, thus enabling a person to live a holy life. Sanctification occurs through the power of God when a person has consecrated himself entirely to God and believed in faith for this transformative experience. They do not believe it is one's own efforts that sanctify an individual, but it is in the complete, humble surrender of one's life as a living sacrifice to God. Faith then appropriates this gift of God. Humble trust in God is the key to receiving every blessing from God, including salvation, sanctification, and all aspects of the daily walk with Christ.

In addition, there are four basic principles regarding behavior in which the conservatives are distinctive. These principles must be defended to outsiders. They are:

- The necessity of keeping the Christian Sabbath.
- The distinction between men and women in clothing and hairstyle.
- Modesty in dress and opposition to outward adornment.
- Carefulness in entertainment, both in the home and elsewhere

1. Instead of following the Jews in using Saturday as a day of rest and worship, Christians chose Sunday as their day of worship in honor of the resurrection on that day (Acts 20:7; Rev 1:10). Adam would have started his week with the Sabbath. Since Adam was created on the sixth day, this would have been man's first full day. The first Christian emperor, Constantine, in AD 321, made a decree that "all judges, city-people and craftsmen shall rest on the venerable day of the Sun."[37] From the time of the early church until about the 1960s, keeping the Lord's Day holy was the accepted practice not only in the church but also in Western culture. This concept is enshrined in the Ten Commandments and was established by God at creation when he "blessed the seventh day, and sanctified it." The CHM still believes in keeping this day as set apart for God.

2. Conservatives adhere to the passages which state, "The woman shall not wear that which pertaineth unto a man" (Deut 22:5), and "If a man have long hair, it is a shame unto him, but if a woman have long hair,

---

37. Byfield, *Christians*, 3:167.

it is a glory to her" (1 Cor 11:14-15). Conservatives emphasize there should be a distinction in the clothing styles and hair length between women and men. The principle, however, is based upon God's creative design by making Adam and Eve male and female. In today's culture, when transgenderism has led to so much confusion regarding gender, it should be an easy argument for conservatives to reemphasize the necessity of clear-cut distinctions between men and women.

3. Conservatives have tried to determine what is modest or immodest in clothing styles. Much of this can be debated, but what is clear is the current styles worn by those of the world are not acceptable. This same immodest clothing is also worn by many in the larger church world. Bathing suits worn down at the beach by even many professing Christians are immodest. All who are trying to live holy would certainly agree. The issue over jewelry and adornment relates to whether some New Testament commands are culturally relative, or should Scripture be kept literally as it was written? Conservatives emphasize that they are simply trying to keep biblical principles (1 Tim 2:9; 1 Pet 3:3).

4. The area of entertainment has a broad focus throughout all of life. The major focus for conservatives is to live a careful life, avoiding temptation. For that reason, one of the major distinctives in their formation was opposition to the use of television. They feared the power of that technology to mold the minds of the next generation. Carelessness toward sin and addictive behaviors has led to the prevalence of many professing Christians becoming addicted to pornography and other forms of evil.

BASIC BIBLICAL EVANGELISM FOR THE HOLINESS PEOPLE

To successfully grow, the community in which a church is located must know who that church is, what they believe, and why they believe it. This must include a well-articulated and simple defense of the reasons for that church's existence in contrast to the other churches of the area. To fail to defend a church's reason for existence means there will be a continual loss of people to other less conservative groups. More liberal churches, unless they can give people a reason to attend, will lose members of their own congregation—some of whom will quit attending church altogether.

Emphasizing the truth is almost the exclusive message of evangelism in the book of Acts. Peter used Scripture and logic to convict the hearts of the hearers and convince them Christ was their Messiah. Stephen also used an intellectual argument, and "they were not able to resist the wisdom and the spirit by which he spake" (Acts 6:10). Paul evangelized the Jews by reasoning with them out of the Scriptures (Acts 17:2). In their evangelism, the apostles and others were not worried about angering the opposing party. Their major concern was to preach the truth, but it was done boldly. These apostles were only following the same path that had been set before them by John the Baptist and Jesus, our great example. The biblical pattern is clear: "Preach the word . . . reprove, rebuke, exhort with all longsuffering and doctrine" (2 Tim 4:2). The town or city in which a church is located must be filled with biblical doctrine (Acts 5:28). For any denomination to grow, it must aggressively defend its beliefs and practices, even if it condemns the sins of the people in the modern churches of today.

Some might suggest we live in a different culture today and the style which was effective in the New Testament will no longer work today. We must recognize that cultures do change and much of the methodology which worked in the past may not be effective today. Yet, the church today is crumbling. Modern methods are not working. Some are doing better than others, but it seems most evangelical and Holiness groups are caught in the same death spiral.

Evangelism based upon defending intellectual ideas is working today, but often it is among those identified as far from mainstream Christianity. Groups such as the Seventh-day Adventists, who emphasize Saturday worship, and United Pentecostals, who do not accept the Trinity, evangelize based upon their differences in theology, and both are very successful. Whether their doctrine is incorrect or not does not seem to hinder them. "People in general may be repelled, but there are a few—perhaps one in a hundred or one in a thousand—who hunger and thirst after what the Saving Remnant has to offer, and by the accession of these few it will grow."[38] If these groups can evangelize utilizing false doctrines, it should be possible for those who have the truth to take it to the people of our world and convince others. Scripture always has the answer for any age. It is time to go back to the Bible and do what they did. Everywhere the apostles went, they successfully convinced some people intellectually that Jesus was the Christ, the Son of God.

Genuine radical Christianity should be ripe to overcome its lack of growth. According to studies by George Barna, "Few areas of lifestyle, apart from religious involvement, make Christians discernible from non-Christians."[39] Society has become disillusioned with religion because nomi-

---

38. Kelley, *Why Conservative Churches Are Growing*, 95.
39. Barna, *Barna Report*, 123.

nal Christianity seems to have little to offer. Only 8 percent of "Christians" profess to keep the Ten Commandments.[40] Problems such as divorce, child rebellion, teenage pregnancy, child abuse, gambling, and other social ills are sweeping rampant across the church world. These problems are rare in some Holiness circles. As the morals of other churches continue to collapse, the stable homes and moral lives of those in Holiness circles will attract those from outside the movement who are looking for stability. Religious history moves in cycles of decline and then revival. The disillusionment found in the world shows society is ready for another general trend toward revival. Societal changes may also bring renewal to the Holiness people. Economic collapse or persecution would cause those in the church and the world to turn toward God. Current trends would suggest the commitment and dedication of Holiness people should place them in the ideal position to impact the world.

---

40. Barna, *Barna Report*, 119.

CHAPTER 16

Hope for the Future

Things do look bleak for the American church, along with Christianity for all of Europe; but the church has overcome many battles before this time, and it will once again be victorious. Decline and renewal of the church has happened repeatedly across history. New life and spiritual depth will one day be restored in Christ's church. I want to be part of that renewal. However, never before has the church in the West sunk as low as it has today. People have always believed in God; yet today, atheism and other religions are making huge inroads into the culture of Europe and America. I have hope for the historic heartland of Western Christianity; but if revival does not come to the West, the church will die in this area. God will continue to advance elsewhere in the world, and his church will continue marching on with or without our country or Europe.

I do recognize we are living on the brink of the second coming of Jesus Christ. Christ predicted dark days before his return, but just because God knew and prophesied the great falling away does not mean he predestined the decline of the church in our day. God simply knew of the lukewarmness of this time. Accordingly, any person, church, denomination, region, or country can have revival and grow if the people will pay the price for revival and trust God. The following are a number of reasons why everyone should be encouraged and believe in a bright hope for the future.

CHRIST SAID, "I WILL BUILD MY CHURCH" (MATT 16:18)

The future of the church does not lie in the power of man but upon the promise given by Jesus Christ. He said, "I will build my church; and the gates of hell shall not prevail against it" (Matt 16:18). The only question is: Will we be part of his church or not? Other areas have completely lost the faith they once held. The original heartland of Christianity—Israel, the Middle East, and North Africa—where Christianity was founded and the areas to which it first spread, have few Christians as a percentage of the population. The next heartland of Christianity, Europe, is in the process of leaving its Christian faith and becoming atheistic. However, Christianity has gone worldwide and is exploding in South America, Africa, and parts of Asia. If our country does lose its faith, Christianity will continue its march, with or without America.

The two times the church might have seemed to decline were AD 600–800 and the rise of secularism in modern times. In the first example, when the Muslims took the Middle East and North Africa, most of the areas that were conquered still had a Christian majority for several centuries. There was not an immediate extinction of Christianity in these areas, but a slow decline. Concurrent with the loss of the Muslim region was the expansion of Christianity both to the north and east across Europe. Yes, there were losses, but also great gains. The other dark day for the church is the last century. Communism for a time seemed to triumph over Christianity, but the church has come through that challenge victoriously. Secularism is presenting another challenge; but without offering any fulfillment for the basic spiritual and social needs for man, it too will eventually fail.

Another current difficulty the church is facing is the explosion of the population in the non-Christian world. In spite of this, it seems that as a percentage of world population, Christianity has held about steady or has only declined slightly.[1] The major competitor to Christianity is the rising Muslim population. Muslim countries have a high fertility rate, and the populations of many of these countries may double over the next several decades, while the populations of many Christian countries are not gaining or are even in decline. In Europe, the population is in decline in most countries, but each country has a Muslim minority which is rapidly growing. If the trends

---

1. In Brierly, *Atlas of World Christianity*, 15, the percentage of Christians in the world has dropped from 30 percent in 1960 to 27 percent in 2010. In *World Almanac and Book of Facts 2019*, 698, the percentage of Christians has stayed about even, with 33 percent of the people of the world claiming Christianity. According to http://global-religiousfutures.org/religions/christians, the growth of Christianity is expected to keep up with rising population and stay steady at 31 percent.

continue, at some point many European countries will have a Muslim majority. Worldwide, the number of Muslims may at some point pass the number of those who are identified as Christians. However, let us never become bound by fear. God has always continued to build his church. Future predictions are often wrong. We can somewhat accurately analyze current events, but things can change in the future. Tomorrow is in the hands of the almighty God, so why should we fear?

GOD'S WORKINGS THROUGHOUT PAST CENTURIES

Over the last six hundred years, each century has begun with a very depressing outlook for the church. In AD 1400, the church was mired in the Great Schism, and the reformation begun by Wycliffe was being squelched in England. The Great Schism ended in 1415, and Wycliffe's reformation continued to be propagated by lay preachers, the Lollards. Wycliffe's ideas were picked up by John Huss in Bohemia, and it led to a revitalized church throughout that country.

In 1500, the church was overwhelmed by both corruption and immorality. The common people had lost faith in the moral character of the church leaders. In the 1490s, Savonarola had led a great revival in Florence, Italy; but the pope was able to have him executed, and the revival fires had died. It looked hopeless; but God had a monk, Martin Luther, whom he was preparing. Only about twenty years later, the ninety-five theses were posted on the doors of the Wittenberg Church, and the Reformation had begun.

By 1600, the fervency of the Reformation had waned, and a Roman Catholic resurgence under the Counter-Reformation had begun. Instead of taking new land, Protestantism was on the defense everywhere in Europe. In England, a semi-Catholic Anglicanism had gained control, and the Stuart dynasty was vehemently opposed to the Puritans in England and the Presbyterians in Scotland. France, which had seemed ready to fall into Protestant hands, had been taken by a secularized Catholicism. In 1618, the Thirty Years' War began with the goal of destroying Protestantism in Bohemia, Germany, and the Netherlands. Overall, the first twenty-five years of the 1600s would at times have looked hopeless to Protestants living then. Catholics crushed the Protestants in Bohemia, now the modern Czech Republic, during the first part of the Thirty Years' War, and gained the upper hand in Germany; however, by mid-century, Protestants had stopped the Catholics in Germany and had gained their freedom in the Netherlands. In England, King Charles I was executed, and the Calvinists gained control.

God had even bigger plans for the 1600s; he was laying the groundwork for the future. The problems in England led to a major migration of Puritans to New England, laying the foundation for much of the greatness of the future United States. The Pietists in Germany and the Quakers in England both helped to recapture a personal relationship with God and a drive for holiness of life. Later the Pietists helped to establish foreign missions, and the Quakers had a great influence upon establishing religious freedom and abolishing slavery.

The 1700s began with a dead church both in England and in America. Millions of slaves were forcibly taken from Africa and sent to the New World. Preachers in New England preached messages called jeremiads constantly warning people, but evil was growing on every side. Harvard University, the college founded by the Puritans, became liberal. The American South had little evangelical religion, began oppressing the poor, and turned to slavery for workers. Quakers lost their zeal and became materialistically minded. In England, the common person was often an alcoholic who spent much of his time in the local pub. Among the English aristocracy, homosexuality was common; and immorality abounded on every side. Society in England may have been equal to its most immoral condition since it had been Christianized. The church, likewise, in 1700, may have been in the worst moral condition of any time since the Reformation. Everything looked hopeless.

It was a number of years before a change began. The Moravians in Germany, under Count Nicholaus von Zinzendorf, by the 1730s began the first Protestant mission works of modern times; and then John Wesley in mid-century began in Great Britain what became the Methodist Church. One of the members of Wesley's inner circle, George Whitefield, came to the American colonies and began traveling throughout the colonies, evangelizing. Others, such as Jonathan Edwards, were already seeing revival. The Great Awakening completely transformed the American church by mid-century. It also had a major impact upon bringing revivalistic religion to the South under the Baptists and Presbyterians. Later, Methodists from England arrived and made a major difference, especially on the frontier. The moving of God during this time and the following century may well have been the greatest and most powerful in history.

Yet, by 1800, all was not going well. The impact of the Enlightenment along with its deistic beliefs and antagonism against religion was at its peak. France was in the throes of the French Revolution, and some Enlightenment leaders were attempting to eradicate Christianity from that country. French military victories led to the spread of their anti-God philosophy throughout Europe. For a time England stood alone, and the people of the country were terrified they would be France's next victim. Even in America, religion seemed to be declining among the major denominations. War normally has a negative impact upon religion, and the revolution devastated the Anglicans; but the Puritans, Presbyterians, and the Methodists had their difficulties also. Yet the Second Great Awakening, which began at Cane Ridge, Kentucky in 1801, along with revival at Yale University, was the start of perhaps the greatest century in Christian history since the apostolic days.

The beginning of the twentieth century saw the impact of religious liberalism, the theory of evolution, and the abandonment of Scripture as the inerrant word of God. Holiness people were under pressure to either leave the Methodist Church or to abandon their doctrine. World War I changed the outlook of the world from a positive outlook to one of pessimism. Bright hopes of science solving all problems and democratic government ending all war was a common thought, but the casualties from World War I and the failure to achieve permanent peace followed by the Great Depression permanently changed the optimistic outlook of the West.

However, the church once again overcame those dark days. The fundamentalists rose to challenge the liberalism of that day, and evangelicals began organizing together. Holiness proponents and the Pentecostal movement established new denominations which began to grow rapidly. In the second half of the twentieth century the story has been all about the rise of these Bible-believing groups. Almost unnoticed has been the incredible expansion of the church into formerly pagan countries in Africa and Asia, and into the Catholic countries of Central and South America.

Now, in the twenty-first century, there are once again fears which could overwhelm Christians. The philosophical change from the modern scientific method to the emotionalism of postmodernism provides a new challenge. The United States is quickly moving away from Christian morality, and even political issues challenging the basic values of the American political system are being debated. Immigration is changing the ethnic context of the American culture. It is a new day with different but equally difficult battles. So what has changed? It seems that at the beginning of each of the last several centuries impossible circumstances were overwhelming the church; however, God has always come through—he will again.

GOD WILL FIGHT FOR AMERICA

Those who hate God and are antagonistic to the truth in many ways do have the upper hand in our country at the present. America will continue to deteriorate morally and spiritually, but all of this leaves God out of the equation. God's plans are far more important than all of the noise the agnostics make. God is in control, and he will make an effort to bring America back to him. We do not know what form these efforts may take, but God will not let America go without a fight. A person only has to look at the nation of Israel as an example. God fought to bring Israel back to him. In the book of Judges, God repeatedly used oppression to bring about repentance and subsequent restoration to his people. When the kings failed to serve God, his nation was carried away into captivity. After the Restoration, the Jewish people never again plunged into idolatry but have maintained their identity as the chosen people of God.

I am convinced the United States was also established by God in a similar fashion as Israel. Our founders personally believed God was directly involved in our founding. Certainly this country became a refuge for persecuted Christians whose major purpose was to worship God. Those founders created a culture in America based upon the Bible, and revival has repeatedly swept across our land. Because of America's efforts to serve God and evangelize the world, the United States has become the most blessed nation in history, and in many ways has become a great blessing to the entire world.

God would far rather pour out benefits upon our country than to bring difficulty. America will be brought back to God, although there may be dark days ahead; but God will do whatever it takes. One of the first steps may be the persecution of the true church. Those who take their stand for God are already being marginalized in society. Freedom of religion means nothing to those who oppose Christians over their position that gay marriage or transgender behavior is wrong. Christians are ordered to abandon their convictions and accept whatever is politically correct or suffer the consequences. The church is facing a rising vehement antagonism in the American culture against biblical morality. If trends continue, it will not be long until Christians will be imprisoned just for speaking the truth against the sin in our world. When faced with persecution, those with genuine convictions will be forced to deepen their prayer life and trust God. No power on earth can withstand the power of praying saints. When the church begins to pray, God will come in his power. The church will be purified, and sinners will once again be convicted and turn to God for salvation.

Another option God may use is problems or disasters. The most likely is military defeat or devastation. In 2001, New York City and Washington, DC suffered major calamity at the hands of Islamic terrorists. It may have been a wake-up call from God. It certainly did expose how helpless our country is when faced with a determined, coordinated attack. If God allows it, the next major incident may be a nuclear bomb or other weapon of mass destruction. Other possibilities include an economic meltdown or a natural disaster of massive proportions. While a person should not usually consider a normal natural disaster as being a direct punishment from God, this tactic has often been used by God in the past. Liberal activists will always blame another alternative, but as Christians we should be concerned that this may be the direct intervention of God.

GOD'S WORKINGS AROUND THE WORLD

The greatest story that is missed by the modern media today is the rapid conversion of third world countries to the Christian faith. One hundred years ago many of these countries were almost untouched by the Christian faith, but today a large number of these countries have over half of the population identifying as Christian, especially in Africa. Many other countries have a sharply rising Christian minority, such as China. South and Central America have a large and rapidly growing evangelical base. If after repeated attempts by God to bring us to revival the United States still rejects God, he may eventually abandon our country; but the church will continue without us in other countries. The heartland of Christianity may change, but the kingdom of God is marching on. However, we should anticipate that America will repent, turn back to God, and revival power will once again sweep our country. America's churches have faced decline before as denominations have lost God; but the true church continues to grow, sometimes within or sometimes outside of those denominations. The church that is being built by God will continue. God will restore the power of his church in this country, and also he is certainly moving throughout the world.

Bibliography

Abraham, William J. "The End of Wesleyan Theology." *Wesleyan Theological Journal* 40:1 (2005) 18–21.
Andros, Paul C. *Wesley's World Parish*. Salem, OH: Schmul, 1980.
Atnip, Mike. *How the Methodists Saved America*. 2003. elcristianismoprimitivo.com/howmethodistssaved.htm.
Avery, Michael, and Larry Smith. *The Call: Essays to the Conservative Holiness Movement* Cincinnati: Revivalist, 2013.
Bailey, Sarah Pulliam. "Christianity Faces Sharp Decline as Americans Are Becoming Even Less Affiliated with Religion." *Washington Post*, May 12, 2015. washingtonpost.com/news/acts-of-faith/wp/2015/05/12/christianity-faces-sharp-decline-as-americans-are-becoming-even-less-affiliated-with-religion/?tid=sm_fb Bailey.
Barna, George. *The Barna Report: 1992–1993*. Ventura, CA: Regal, 1992.
———. *Future Cast: What Today's Trends Mean for Tomorrow's World*. Tyndale, 2011.
Batalova, Jeanne, et al. "Frequently Requested Statistics on Immigrants and Immigration in the United States." *Migration Policy Institute*, February 14, 2020. https://www.migrationpolicy.org/article/frequently-requested-statistics-immigrants-and-immigration-united-states
Bernstein, Douglas A., and Peggy W. Nash. *Essentials of Psychology*. New York: Houghton Mifflin, 2008.
Bible Missionary Church. *Fourteenth General Conference Journal*. Springdale, AR: 2003.
Black, Brian. *The Holiness Heritage*. Salem, OH: Allegheny, 2003.
Black, Robert, and Keith Drury. *The Story of the Wesleyan Church*. Indianapolis: Wesleyan, 2012.
Blanchard, John, and Dan Lucarini. *Can We Rock the Gospel?* Webster, NY: Evangelical, 2006.
Brierley, Peter, and Heather Wraight. *Atlas of World Christianity: 2000 Years*. Nashville: Thomas Nelson, 1998.
Bushart, W. David. *Exploring Protestant Traditions*. Downers Grove, IL: InterVarsity, 2006.
Byfield, Ted, ed. *The Christians: Their First Two Thousand Years*. Vol. 3: *By This Sign*. 12 vols. Edmonton, AB: McCallum, 2003.
Calvin, John. *Calvin's Commentary on the Bible*. https://www.studylight.org/commentaries/cal/1-john-3.html.

———. *Institutes of the Christian Religion*. Original edition, 1559. Translated by Henry Beveridge. s.l.: Calvin Translation Society, 1845. https://ccel.org/ccel/calvin/institutes/institutes.v.iii.html.

Carpenter, Alexander. "Adventist Church Reports Second Highest Growth among Denominations in North America." *Spectrum*, February 17, 2011. https://spectrummagazine.org/article/alexander-carpenter/2011/02/17/adventist-church-reports-second-highest-growth-among-denomina. Church of the Nazarene.

Church of the Nazarene Manual 2017–2021. Kansas City: Nazarene, 2017.

Cloud, David. "The Church Growth Movement: An Analysis of Rick Warren's *Purpose Driven Church*." wayoflife.org/database/growthstrategy.html.

Cook, Arnold. *Historical Drift*. Camp Hill, PA: Christian, 2000.

Corner, Daniel D. *The Believer's Conditional Security*. Washington, PA: Evangelical Outreach, 2000.

Dickerson, John S. *The Great Evangelical Recession*. Grand Rapids: Baker, 2013.

Driscoll, Mark. *A Call to Resurgence*. Carol Stream, IL: Tyndale, 2013.

Drury, Keith, et al. *Counterpoint: Dialogue with Drury on the Holiness Movement*. Salem, OH: Schmul, 2005.

Duewel, Wesley L. *Heroes of the Holy Life*. Grand Rapids: Zondervan, 2002.

———. *Revival Fire*. Grand Rapids: Zondervan, 1995.

Finke, Roger, and Rodney Stark. *The Churching of America, 1776–1990*. Brunswick, NJ: Rutgers University Press, 1992.

———. "Demographics of Religious Participation: An Ecological Approach, 1850–1980." *Journal for the Scientific Study of Religion* 28 (1989) 45–58.

Flatt, Kevin N., et al. "Secularization and Attribution: How Mainline Protestant Clergy and Congregants Explain Church Growth and Decline." *Sociology of Religion* 79:1 (2018). https://academic.oup.com/socrel/article-abstract/79/1/78/4563828.

Galli, Mark, and Ted Olsen. *131 Christians Everyone Should Know*. Nashville: Broadman & Holman, 2000.

Glick, Jerald. "I'm Contending for the Glory." *Sing & Rejoice*. Westfield, IN: Glick and Victory, 1995.

Godbey, William B. *Holiness or Hell*. Noblesville, IN: Newby Book Room, 1974.

Grossman, Cathy Lynn. "Why Some Evangelicals Changed Their Minds about Evolution." *Religion News Service*, June 11, 2016. https://religionnews.com/2016/06/11/why-some-evangelicals-changed-their-minds-about-evolution/.

Haines, Lee M., and Paul William Thomas. *An Outline History of the Wesleyan Church*. 5th ed. Indianapolis: Wesleyan, 2000.

Ham, Ken, and Britt Beemer. *Already Gone: Why Your Kids Will Quit Church and What You Can Do to Stop It*. Green Forest, AR: Master, 2009.

Hardman, Keith J. *Seasons of Refreshing*. Grand Rapids: Baker, 1994.

Hatfield, John T. *Thirty-Three Years a Live Wire*. Shoals, IN: Old Paths Tract Society, n.d.

Hodges, Sam. "Immigrants Bringing Charismatic Flavor to U.S. Catholicism." *The Dallas Morning News*, May 24, 2007. https://www.dallasnews.com/news/faith/2007/05/24/immigrants-bringing-charismatic-flavor-to-u-s-catholicism/.

Hunter, George G., III. *To Spread the Power: Church Growth in the Wesleyan Spirit*. Nashville: Abingdon, 1987.

Hyles, Jack. *Enemies of Soul Winning*. Hammond, IN: Hyles-Anderson, 1993.

Iannaccone, Laurence R. "Why Strict Churches are Strong." *American Journal of Sociology* 99:5 (1994) 1180–1211.

———. "Sacrifice and Stigma: Reducing Free-riding in Cults, Communes, and Other Collectives." *Journal of Political Economy* 100.2 (April 1992) 271–91.

"John Calvin on Antinomianism and the Perseverance of the Saints." www.bcbsr.com/topics/calvantip.html.

Jones, E. O. Jack. "Sand and Sinning Saints." *Faith in the Future* 38:4 (Fall 2009) 7–21.

Kelley, Dean M. *Why Conservative Churches Are Growing*. New York: Harper & Row, 1972.

Lawson, J. Gilchrist. *Deeper Experiences of Famous Christians*. Uhrichville, OH: Barbour, 1999.

Loritts, Bryan. "A Life-Changing Question." *Didaktikos* (September 2019) 48–49.

Marshall, Peter, and David Manuel. *The Light and the Glory*. Tarrytown, NY: Revell, 1977.

McBeth, H. Leon. *The Baptist Heritage: Four Centuries of Baptist Witness*. Nashville: Broadman, 1987.

McBride, Michael. "Why Churches Need Free-Riders: Religious Capital Formation and Religious Group Survival." *Journal of Behavioral and Experimental Economics* 58:2 (2015) 77–87.

McChesney, Audine. *Through Congo Shadows*. Hobe Sound, FL: The Print Shop, 1968.

McDowell, Josh, and Bob Hostetler. *The New Tolerance*. Wheaton, IL: Tyndale, 1998.

McMillan, Dan. "Hitler, Darwin and the Holocaust: How the Nazis Distorted the Theory of Evolution." *Salon*, April 19, 2014. https://www.salon.com/2014/04/19/charles_darwins_tragic_error_hitler_evolution_racism_and_the_holocaust/.

Mooshian, C. Helen. *His Ambassador*. Shoals, IN: Old Paths Tract Society, 1990.

Niebuhr, Richard. *The Social Sciences of Denominationalism*. New York: New American Library, 1957.

Olasky, Marvin. "Creative Philanthropy." *World*, September 14, 2019. https://world.wng.org/2019/08/creative_philanthropy.

Olson, David T. *The American Church in Crisis*. Grand Rapids: Zondervan, 2008.

Pew Research Center. "Changing Faiths: Latinos and the Transformation of American Religion." https://www.pewresearch.org/hispanic/2007/04/25/ii-religion-and-demography/.

Purkiser, W. T. *Called Unto Holiness*. Vol. 2. 2 vols. Kansas City: Nazarene, 1983.

Quanstrom, Mark. *A Century of Holiness Theology*. Kansas City: Beacon Hill, 2004.

Raynold, Prosper. "An Economic Theory of Religious Affiliation." Miami University, Oxford, OH, October 2017. https://www.researchgate.net/publication/320566441_AN_ECONOMIC_THEORY_OF_RELIGIOUS_AFFILIATION.

Roozen, David A., and C. Kirk Hadaway. *Church and Denominational Growth*. Nashville: Abingdon, 1993.

Ryrie, Charles. *So Great Salvation: What It Means to Believe in Jesus Christ*. Wheaton, IL: Victor, 1989.

Schaeffer, Francis A. *The Great Evangelical Disaster*. Westchester, IL: Crossway, 1984.

Sine, Tom. "A Wakeup Call for Evangelicals." *Patheos*, August 8, 2010. https://www.patheos.com/resources/additional-resources/2010/08/a-wakeup-call-for-evangelicals.

Smith, Christian. *American Evangelicalism: Embattled and Thriving*. Chicago: University of Chicago Press, 1998.

Stark, Rodney. *The Rise of Christianity*. New York: Harper Collins, 1996.

"Startling Facts: An Up-Close Look at Church Attendance in America." *Outreach Magazine*, April 10, 2018.https://churchleaders.com/pastors/pastor-articles/139575-7-startling-facts-an-up-close-look-at-church-attendance-in-america.html.

Stetzer, Ed. "The Southern Baptist Decline Continues—and Accelerates." *Between the Times*, June 11, 2015. http://betweenthetimes.com/index.php/2015/06/11/the-southern-baptist-decline-continues/.

———. "Why Do These Pentecostals Keep Growing?" *Christianity Today*, November 11, 2014. https://www.christianitytoday.com/edstetzer/2014/november/why-are-pentecostals-growing.html.

Strobel, Lee. *The Case for Faith*. Grand Rapids: Zondervan, 2000.

Sweet, William Warren. *Revivalism in America: Its Origin, Growth and Decline*. New York: Scribner's Sons, 1944.

Terrill, Joseph Goodwin. *The Life of Rev. John Wesley Redfield, M. D.* Titusville, PA: Allegheny Wesleyan Methodist, n.d.

Thomas, Jeremy N., and Daniel V. A. Olson. "Testing the Strictness Thesis and Competing Theories of Congregational Growth." *Journal for the Scientific Study of Religion* 49:4 (2010) 619–39.

Tipple, Ezra Squier. *Francis Asbury: The Prophet of the Long Road*. Nicholasville, KY: Schmul, 2007.

Torrance, David Wishart, et al. *John 11–21 and 1 John*. Torrance Edition. Grand Rapids: Eerdmans, 1994.

Tredoux, Johan. *Mildred Bangs Wynkoop: Her Life and Thought*. Kansas City: Nazarene, 2017.

Twenge, Jean M. *iGen*. New York: Atria, 2017.

———. "Our Changing Culture." *Psychology Today* 5 (2015). https://www.psychologytoday.com/us/blog/our-changing-culture/201505/the-real-reason-religion-is-declining-in-america.

Veith, Gene Edward, Jr. *Postmodern Times: A Christian Guide to Contemporary Thought and Culture*. Wheaton, IL: Crossway, 1994.

Wallace, O. C. S. *What Baptists Believe*. 1913. Reprint. Piqua, OH: Calvary Baptist Church, 2000.

Wesley, John. *The Works of John Wesley, Vol. 1*. 14 vols. Grand Rapids: Baker, 2007.

White, James Emery. *Rise of the Nones*. Grand Rapids: Baker, 2014.

The World Almanac and Book of Facts 2019. New York: Infobase, 2018.

Zahniser, Clarence Howard. *Earnest Christian: Life and Works of Benjamin Titus Roberts*. Circleville, OH: Advocate, 1957.

Zong, Jie, et al. "Frequently Requested Statistics on Immigrants and Immigration in the United States in 2016." *Migration Policy Institute*, February 8, 2018. https://www.migrationpolicy.org/article/frequently-requested-statistics-immigrants-and-immigration-united-states-2016.

Zuckerman, Phil. "Christianity Declining, Secularism Rising." *Psychology Today* 5 (2015). psychologytoday.com/us/blog/the-secular-life/201505/christianity-declining-secularism-rising.

www.ingramcontent.com/pod-product-compliance
Lightning Source LLC
Chambersburg PA
CBHW070916160426
43193CB00011B/1476